The Vocation of Service to God and Neighbour

International Medieval Research
Selected Proceedings of the International Medieval Congress
University of Leeds

International Medieval Research

The Vocation of Service to God and Neighbour

Essays on the Interests, Involvements and Problems of Religious Communities and their Members in Medieval Society

Selected Proceedings of the
International Medieval Congress
University of Leeds
14-17 July 1997

edited by
Joan Greatrex

Turnhout, Brepols
1998

Articles appearing in this volume are indexed in
"International Medieval Bibliography"

Printed in Belgium
D/1998/0095/34
ISBN 2-503-50741-7

Contents

Foreword

Seven of the nine papers collected in this volume were read by their authors at the fourth annual International Medieval Congress sponsored by the University of Leeds in 1997. Of the remainder, one became stranded on the M1, with its author, only hours before it was due to be delivered and the other was at the time still in progress. It is a gratifying conclusion for the participants in the sessions and also for their organiser to see the papers now made available to a wider audience.

The publication of these essays provides an opportunity to draw the attention of research students and scholars to several important areas in the field of ecclesiastical and monastic history in the medieval period: areas in which there is ample scope for further investigation. Their extent is broadly suggested by the title chosen for the volume and is more specifically delineated in the subtitle, but a brief word of explanation is in order by way of elucidating the theme.

At the core of what is generally described as the religious vocation there is a personal commitment to a life wholly devoted to serving God, usually within a community and under a prescribed rule. A significant portion of each day is given to communal prayer and worship in which the liturgy of the office and eucharist play the central role. The daily readings at these services are charged with constant reminders of the second great commandment, that of loving and serving God in one's neighbour: a neighbour who is to be found not only in the cloister but also in the world outside. Separation from the world has never eliminated the responsibility of service to others, and the nuns, monks and friars of the later middle ages played their part not only in supporting their friends and benefactors through their continual round of prayer, but also in offering hospitality and alms to all who sought them. In addition monks and, more especially, friars taught, preached and carried out other pastoral duties as required. It is a distorted view that dismisses the inhabitants of medieval monasteries and convents as spineless men and women retreating from the harsh realities of secular life or pities them as having little alternative in the era in which it was their lot to live. This attitude is one that judges them incapable of choosing a way of life prompted by the sincere conviction that they had received a call. The degree of their success or failure in living up to the spiritual ideal set before them is, with respect to this judgement, irrelevant; human nature is no less frail now than it was then.

The interests, involvements and problems of the medieval religious whose careers are studied in these essays furnish abundant evidence of their regular contacts with other religious and with clergy and laity; they also illustrate the varying reactions and responses on both sides. Two of the papers, for example, offer fresh perspectives on the lives of individual monks, with a scrutiny of the roots of Robert Joseph's humanism and a reassessment of John Lydgate's pastoral undertakings. Again, the study devoted to Westwood nunnery benefits from the recent recovery of archival records that shed light on its administration and lay personnel. New research has also shaped the authors' approaches to the uneasy relations between thirteenth century Benedictine monks and Franciscan friars and to the challenge presented by lay spiritual movements to the Dominicans in the fourteenth century. That the later medieval abbey of St Albans was a flourishing centre of learning has been confirmed beyond doubt by the evidence laid before us in one of two papers dealing with intellectual pursuits; the other, also based on new research, is a comparative study of the members of religious orders who were registered in the theological faculty of the university of Paris. Finally, two contributions, both based on current and ongoing research, explore in depth the trauma of the 1530s for English monks and nuns. Here, then, is a diversity of topics held together by an underlying unity of theme.

I should like to express my thanks to the contributors for their continuing cooperation at every stage in the preparation of this volume. As our sponsor at the Congress, we were honoured to have the Borthwick Institute of Historical Research with the kind permission of its director, Professor David Smith. Occasional sagacious comments from Dame Catherine Wybourne, O. S. B. have rescued me from more than one impasse in my editorial role. To Amanda Banton for her initial encouragement of this enterprise and for her immediate and unfailing response to all my requests whenever a problem arose I now, with pleasure, acknowledge my debt of gratitude.

Joan Greatrex

Notes on Authors

James Clark is a lecturer in modern history at St Edmund Hall, Oxford and his research is focused on monastic learning in late medieval England.

Peter Cunich is a lecturer in history at the University of Hong Kong and director of the Monastic Database project.

Margaret Goodrich read history at Cambridge and has since taught in both secondary schools and continuing education programmes for adults.

Nicholas Heale is a priest in the diocese of Leicester whose doctoral thesis dealt with the spiritual and intellectual life of the monks of Bury St Edmunds.

Anthony Marett-Crosby is a Benedictine monk of Ampleforth Abbey at present engaged in graduate studies at Oxford.

Marilyn Oliva is currently affiliated with Fordham University, New York and is a member of the editorial board of the journal *Medieval Prosopography*.

Michael Robson is a Franciscan friar (O. F. M. Conv.) and is the Dean of St Edmund's College, Cambridge.

Walter Senner is a Dominican friar and the regent of studies at the Dominikanerkloster in Cologne.

Thomas Sullivan is a Benedictine monk of Conception Abbey, Missouri whose interests centre on late medieval French monastic history and the history of the late medieval university.

Joan Greatrex retired from the history department of Carleton University, Ottawa and is currently affiliated with Robinson College, Cambridge.

Abbreviations

BL	London, British Library
CUL	Cambridge, University Library
Oxford, Bod.	Oxford, Bodleian Library
PRO	London, Public Record Office

Dugdale, *Monasticon*	W. Dugdale, *Monasticon Anglicanum*, rev. edn by J. Caley, H. Ellis and B. Bandinel, 6 vols in 8 (London, 1817-30).
Gasquet, *Henry VIII and the English Monasteries*	F. A. Gasquet, *Henry VIII and the English Monasteries* (London, 1925).
Harvey, *Living and Dying*	Barbara Harvey, *Living and Dying in England, 1100-1540: The Monastic Experience* (Oxford, 1993).
Hodgett, "Unpensioned Ex-religious"	G. A. J. Hodgett, "The Unpensioned Ex-religious in Tudor England", *Journal of Ecclesiastical History*, 13 (1962), 195-202.
Knowles, *Religious Orders*	David Knowles, *The Religious Orders in England*, 3 vols (Cambridge, 1948-59).
Letters and Papers, Henry VIII	*Letters and Papers, Foreign and Domestic, Henry VIII*, 21 vols and 2 addenda (London, 1864-1932).
Pantin, *Black Monk Chapters*	W. Pantin, ed., *Documents illustrating the Activities of the General and Provincial Chapters of the English Black Monks, 1215-1540*, 3 vols, Camden Society, 3rd series, 45(1), 47(2), 54(3) (London, 1931-37).
Rule of St Benedict, (*RB 1980*)	Timothy Fry, ed., *RB 1980: The Rule of St Benedict* (Collegeville, 1980).
Valor Ecclesiasticus	J. Caley and J. Hunter, eds, *Valor Ecclesiasticus, temp. Henrici VIII, Auctoritate Regia Institutus*, 6 vols (London, 1810-34).

VCH	*The Victoria History of the Counties of England* (London, 1900-).
Youings, *Dissolution*	Joyce Youings, *The Dissolution of the Monasteries* (London, 1971).

Monachi and Magistri: The Context and Culture of Learning at Late Medieval St Albans*

James Clark

In a short passage in the *Gesta Abbatum sancti Albani*, the chronicler Thomas Walsingham recalls the scholars active at St Albans in his own time:

> In our own day Nicholas Radcliffe has written books condemning the opinions of the heretic John Wyclif, and William Binham too has determined against these opinions. Simon Southerey has also turned many away from the errors of the same John with his preaching: these are all monks of this place, and are Professors of the Sacred Page. Simon is learned in the art of versification (*ars uersificatoria*) is skilled in astronomy and astrology and in the art of poetry (*ars poetria*) is considered the most learned in the whole kingdom ... in recent times, my lord Thomas Hatfield, who was appointed bishop of Durham, was brought up in this monastery. Master

*The following discussion is based on a more detailed examination of the later medieval St Albans books in my "Intellectual Life at the Abbey of St Albans and the Nature of Monastic Learning in England, c. 1350-c. 1440" (unpublished D.Phil. dissertation, University of Oxford, 1997).

> John Barnet was also nurtured from infancy in this place, whence he has risen to hold three prelacies, first in the church of Worcester, then of Bath, then, by papal provision, of Ely.[1]

His recollections reveal a vigorous community of scholars engaged in diverse studies, in theological controversy, literary scholarship, astronomy and even elementary education: in short, an image which historians do not usually associate with English Benedictine communities in the later middle ages. It is a well-established article of faith amongst medieval historians that the cultural and intellectual achievements of the English monasteries in the high middle ages were never matched by their fourteenth- and fifteenth-century successors. William of Malmesbury and Matthew Paris, it is assumed, have no natural late medieval counterparts, except perhaps a small and ever-dwindling number of mediocre annalists and chroniclers; even the histories of Thomas Walsingham himself are often discussed in these terms.[2] These views are founded on a historiographical tradition established in the nineteenth century, which championed the rise of a secular culture in the later middle ages as well as a secular religion; but their origin can be traced back even further to the clamorous allegations of decadence and decline which had attended the dissolution itself.[3]

[1] BL MS Cotton Claudius E iv fol. 334r; H. T. Riley, ed., *Annales monasterii sancti Albani a Iohanne Amundsham*, Rolls Series 28/5 (London, 1870-71), 2:304-5 (henceforth *Amundsham*).

[2] For discussions of English monastic history which emphasise this cultural decline see Knowles, *Religious Orders*, 3:460; Youings, *Dissolution*, pp. 22-23; A. Gransden, *Historical Writing in England c. 1307 to the Early Sixteenth Century* (London, 1982), pp. 465-66; A. G. Dickens, *Late Monasticism and the Reformation* (London, 1991), pp. 74-80. For assessments of Walsingham and his work see V. H. Galbraith, *The St Albans Chronicle, 1406-1422* (Oxford, 1937), pp. xxxvi-xlv; Gransden, *Historical Writing*, pp. 118-56; A. G. Rigg, *A History of Anglo-Latin Literature, 1066-1422* (Cambridge, 1992), pp. 297-98.

[3] For examples of the Victorian views of cultural change in the later middle ages see A. F. Leach, *The Schools of Medieval England* (London, 1915); Gasquet, *Henry VIII and the English Monasteries*, pp. xxvii-xxxv; G. G. Coulton, *Five Centuries of Religion. IV. The Last Days of Medieval Monachism*

Recent historians have done much to rehabilitate the character of monastic life in the later middle ages, emphasising communities' adaptability, administrative efficiency and even the sociability of their relations with the secular world.[4] But the intellectual activities of monks in the fourteenth and fifteenth centuries remain largely neglected. From the 1930s to the 1960s W. A. Pantin recovered abundant source materials, including books, documents, letters and treatises, for a reinterpretation of later medieval monastic learning, but never completed such a study himself.[5] Recent scholars have continued his work in recovering the legacy of the monastic colleges at Oxford and the monk-scholars who studied there, but have not examined in detail their scholarship or their influence on claustral studies in their home communities.[6]

The aim of the following discussion is to offer a broad reassessment of later medieval monastic culture through a brief examination of the activities and interests of the monks at the abbey of St Albans. St Albans was a large, ancient community, distinguished from other communities by its wealth and royal patronage. But as the head of a large, diverse network of smaller communities, it can offer an entry-point into monastic England as a whole. Moreover, its numerous surviving later medieval books and

(Cambridge, 1950). For views contemporary with the dissolution see Knowles, *Religious Orders*, 3:76-80, 306-15; Youings, *Dissolution*, pp. 149-52, 160-65.

[4] R. B. Dobson, *Durham Priory, 1400-1440* (Cambridge, 1973); B. F. Harvey, *Westminster Abbey and its Estates in the Middle Ages* (Oxford, 1977); Harvey, *Living and Dying*; J. H. Tillotson, *Monastery and Society in the Later Middle Ages: Select Accounts from Selby Abbey, Yorkshire, 1398-1537* (Woodbridge, 1988).

[5] Pantin, *Black Monk Chapters*; Pantin, *Canterbury College, Oxford*, Oxford Historical Society 6-8 (1941-44); Pantin, "Some Medieval Treatises on the Origins of Monasticism", in *Medieval Studies Presented to Rose Graham*, ed. V. Ruffner and A. J. Taylor (London, 1950), pp. 189-215.

[6] Dobson, *Durham Priory*, esp. pp. 315-17; B. F. Harvey, "The Monks of Westminster and the University of Oxford", in *The Reign of Richard II: Essays in Honour of May McKisack*, ed. F. R. H. du Boulay and C. M. Barron (London, 1971), pp. 108-30; J. Greatrex, "Monk Students from Norwich Cathedral Priory at Oxford and Cambridge, c. 1300-1530", *English Historical Review* 106 (1991), 555-83.

writings – not least Walsingham's own much annotated copies of the *Gesta* – offer insights into claustral culture not matched in the material which survives from communities elsewhere.[7] The evidence of the books reveals a community much as Walsingham himself recalled it: a centre of education for religious and secular alike, home to a succession of distinguished university graduates. It also demonstrates that there was more to intellectual life at St Albans than the academic interests of a handful of *magistri*: it suggests that the late medieval cloister was an environment where both traditional monastic studies continued to flourish and where also new, independent cultural influences – including the classicism of continental scholars – were absorbed.

From Walsingham's comments it might at first be inferred that the vigour of intellectual life at St Albans was entirely the result of university attendance: the scholars he chooses to commemorate were, he emphasises, "all Professors of the Sacred Page", meaning each had completed the doctorate in theology. However, the surviving books, their form, content and evidence of use, suggest that the real basis of the abbey's intellectual vitality in the fourteenth and fifteenth centuries was in fact the wide range of teaching activities which continued within the cloister itself. In particular, the evidence shows that across the fourteenth and fifteenth centuries the novitiate developed a rigorous programme of training which led most monks into further studies after their profession, whether or not they subsequently studied at the universities. The emergence of this new educational programme was to some extent a response to the 1336 canons *Summi magistri* and the companion statutes of the General Chapter issued in 1343, both of which aimed at a broad reform of monastic education. But in

[7] For manuscripts from St Albans and its cells see N. Ker, *Medieval Libraries of Great Britain. A List of Surviving Books*, 2nd edn (London, 1964), pp. 164-68; Ker and Andrew G. Watson, *Medieval Libraries of Great Britain. A Supplement* (London, 1987), pp. 59-60; G. R. C. Davis, *Medieval Cartularies of Great Britain* (London, 1958), pp. 94-96, 112, 125; R. Sharpe, R. M. Thomson, J. P. Carley, A. G. Watson and K. Friis-Jensen, *English Benedictine Libraries: The Shorter Catalogues*, Corpus of British Medieval Library Catalogues 4 (London, 1996), pp. 554-85.

detail the new St Albans novitiate was the work of a succession of vigorously reformist abbots, including Michael Mentmore (1334-1349) and Thomas de la Mare (1349-1396), whose commitment to a broad range of studies for their monks went further than the official legislation. Under their constitutions, a fixed three-year novitiate was established, newly-professed monks retaining junior status for ten years. The claustral prior was charged with directing the instruction of recruits and *professi*, examining them himself for their knowledge of the Benedictine Rule (*uiua uoce exponat*), while skilled monk scholars and an increasing number of stipendiary secular masters offered a wide range of teaching on other subjects.[8] The full curriculum of studies remains difficult to determine. Undoubtedly, the Rule and its related commentaries and homiletics remained the central focus for newest recruits, but it seems that as they progressed further an increasing amount of their time was devoted to wider studies. The liturgy was certainly considered important, even if it was never formally taught in the cloister: a large number of small-format liturgical books were compiled and copied in the later fourteenth and fifteenth centuries, although it is difficult to connect these in particular with the work of novices.[9] There is firm evidence that newcomers were also taught Latin grammar. Amongst the obituaries of late fourteenth-century monks recorded in the 1440s is William Trent, sub-almoner, said to have taught grammar for several decades and to have been "a profound grammarian, skilled instructor of the monks ... another Donatus". In the later fifteenth century a secular master seems to have been appointed to teach "grammar and other things which it is necessary

[8] H. T. Riley, ed., *Gesta abbatum monasterii sancti Albani a Thoma Walsingham*, Rolls Series 28/4 (London, 1867-68), 2:102-17, 184, 299, 373, 435-54 (henceforth *Gesta abbatum*); Cambridge, Trinity College MS O. 9. 25 fols 161r-65v; H. T. Riley, ed., *Registrum abbatiae Iohannis Whethamstede*, Rolls Series 28/6 (London, 1872-73), 2:68, 89 (henceforth *Registrum Whethamstede*); BL MS Cotton Nero D vii fol. 82r; *Amundsham*, 1:110; Oxford, Jesus College MS 77 fol. 320v.

[9] For liturgical texts see Sharpe, *English Benedictine Libraries*, pp. 554-63; Oxford, Bod. MS Lat. Liturg. g. 8; Oxford, Bod. MS Gough Liturg. 18 fols xviiii v-xvii r; Cambridge, Fitzwilliam Museum MS 274 fols 1r-33v.

for juniors to know".[10] It remains unclear what level of instruction was offered by these masters; a significant number of recruits had attended a grammar school prior to profession and at any rate no newcomer would reach junior status without at least elementary Latin. It is possible that following profession the grammatical studies of new monks were more narrowly focused on the *ars dictaminis*. Walsingham relates in the *Gesta* that Thomas de la Mare spent a year after his profession engaged in the study of "rhetoric and the art of letter writing". There are several rhetorical and dictaminal treatises amongst the surviving books which may have been used in these studies: one such collection combines Thomas of Capua's popular *Ars dictandi* with genuine letters from de la Mare's register.[11] During Walsingham's lifetime, novices and *professi* were also taught music. Walsingham himself wrote a short, elementary treatise on mensurable notation and the use of rests, *Regulae de figuris*, while he served as precentor in the 1380s, written, he observes in the introduction, "since it is necessary for youths to learn music". Walsingham's treatise describes and explains the common note forms using extracts from familiar antiphons and hymns, and judging from the large number of house antiphoners copied in this period, it seems novices were encouraged then to continue their studies in their own time.[12]

Surprisingly, there is no evidence that a claustral *lector* or master was ever permanently established within the community. As is discussed below, monk-graduates tended to assume administrative rather than teaching roles following their return to the cloister. Senior members of the community may have provided teaching on an occasional basis. Walsingham maintained in the *Gesta* that many graduates of his generation had received their earliest instruction from Thomas de la Mare himself, "per ipsum abbatem educati, in diuersis scientiis instructi". There is also some evidence of scholars

[10] BL MS Cotton Nero D vii fols 82v, 149v; *Amundsham*, 1:110, 435-36.

[11] *Gesta abbatum*, 2:374; Cambridge, Clare College MS 14 fols 1r-61r; 85r-92r; CUL MS Ee 4.20 fols 117v-65r.

[12] BL MS Lansdowne 762 fols 98v-105r at 98v. For antiphoners copied at the abbey in the late fourteenth and early fifteenth centuries see Sharpe, *English Benedictine Libraries*, pp. 564-83.

from outside being invited to teach in the cloister; Dr John Waldeby, a distinguished theologian based at the Austin friars convent at York, is known to have visited the cell at Tynemouth during Thomas de la Mare's priorate to lead the monks, in Walsingham's words, "in studio praedicandi uerbum Dei tam in lingua Anglica quam Latina". Generally, however, the later abbots were reluctant to recast the cloister as a thoroughly academic environment dominated by graduate teachers. Indeed, in their sermons, visitation examinations and reform constitutions they appear to have been concerned rather to inspire a return to more traditional forms of individual study; the language of these pronouncements echoes Benedict's Rule, they return again and again to the importance of scripture, homiletics and the Rule itself as core texts, and to the image of the *opus claustralium*, a phrase which is regularly repeated in the inscriptions of the books they donated to the conventual collection.[13]

The importance of the traditional *opus claustralium* to the character of learning at late medieval St Albans was also reflected in the monks' continuing interest and involvement in the copying, correction and decoration of their own books. It has long been assumed that large-scale book production disappeared from even the larger, wealthier monasteries in the fourteenth and fifteenth centuries as communities came to rely on the work of commercial *scriptoria*.[14] Perhaps as many as two-thirds of the books added to the conventual collection at St Albans between 1370 and 1440, however, can be shown to have been the work of the monks themselves. Many of the larger, more complex compilations were produced by a core group of trained monk scribes, but it is clear that as a whole the cloister-monks were all encouraged to develop scribal skills and to be involved in some aspect of work in the *scriptorium*. In his 1351 reform constitutions, Abbot de la Mare

[13] *Gesta abbatum*, 2:380; Oxford, Bod. MS Laud Misc. 296 fol. 57ra; BL MS Cotton Nero D vii fol. 111v.

[14] Knowles, *Religious Orders*, 2:277-79; A. I. Doyle, "Book Production by Members of the Monastic Orders, c. 1375-1530", in *Medieval Book Production: Assessing the Evidence*, ed. L. L. Brownrigg (Los Altos Hills, 1987), pp. 1-19.

drew particular attention to the injunction issued in the 1343 Chapter that cloister monks should occupy themselves 'in writing, copying and illuminating'. Inventories show that writing materials including vellum, ink, and knives for sharpening *styli* were available in every room which was set aside for monastic studies.[15] The homogeneity of the scripts used in the fourteenth- and fifteenth-century manuscripts might even suggest writing was taught in the cloister as part of the newcomer's training. The large number of small-format liturgical books copied in this period indicate that the cloister-monks not only regarded their scribal activities in practical terms but also continued to treat copying as an act of monastic devotion with spiritual benefits comparable to meditation in the cloister or worship in the abbey church. Most of these books are anthologies, containing extracts from the house antiphoner, the psalter and an annotated calendar, evidently intended for personal use; several are also illustrated with images which reflect personal devotional interests, some with depictions of the Virgin, some of Benedict.[16]

In addition to a more rigorous novitiate, the monks at late medieval St Albans were also exposed to learning in non-textual forms. Throughout the conventual buildings the monks, whether obedientiaries burdened with administrative duties, or those with no specific role who moved between cloister and choir, were constantly exposed to images representing a diverse range of concepts and stories. According to a number of later fourteenth-century inventories, the spaces around the altars, the walls of the chapels, the chapter house and the cloister were covered with paintings and inscriptions depicting familiar scriptural passages or stories from the abbey's own annals. In the 1450s Whethamstede developed a scheme of images of Old Testament patriarchs and prophets for the windows in the cloister; each one carried a portrait of a biblical figure together with smaller scenes from their life and short

[15] Cambridge, Trinity College MS O. 9. 25 fols 161r-65v; Pantin, *Black Monk Chapters*, 2:51; CUL MS Ee 4. 20 fol. 273r.

[16] Cambridge, Trinity College MS R. O. 5 fols 177r-93v; Oxford, New College MS 358 fols iv, v-vii r; Oxford, Bod. MS Lat. Liturg. g. 8 fols 68v, 88r, 108r, 132v. See also Sharpe, *English Benedictine Libraries*, pp. 562-64.

versified inscriptions relating their significance to the viewer. Some of these images, however, seem to have been designed to convey more complex ideas: under the conventual clock in the passageway linking the cloister with the abbey church there was an image taken from Isaiah 11.1 and a short inscription relating the allegory, "the flower is Christ, the virgin the mother of God, from whom we are saved the pain of death". These images were concentrated in areas of significance throughout the community, such as the entrance to the chapter-house, the abbots' chamber and the cloister; as such they seem to represent a pragmatic response to the fragmentation of community life, offering an alternative means of instruction as their duties increasingly took the monks away from their carrells in the cloister.[17]

For the majority of the monks at St Albans in the fourteenth and fifteenth centuries the experience of active learning – as distinct from individual studies in chamber, church or cloister – was limited to their time as novices and juniors. Higher studies were probably only ever open to a small minority: for all Walsingham's claims, St Albans was never a community crowded with *magistri*. Prospective monk-students seem to have been identified soon after their admission and often even before the novitiate had been completed. As a community, late-medieval St Albans was dominated by a small, closely-knit hierarchy whose family connections with the abbey had endured over many generations, and it was from this body that the majority of the monk-students were chosen: two of Walsingham's three *magistri*, Binham and Southerey, were members of these dominant St Albans dynasties, as were several of the community's other distinguished graduates such as William Heyworth, abbot from 1401-1420 and John Whethamstede, abbot 1420-1441 and 1452-1465. It was not impossible for recruits lacking these connections to reach Gloucester College, but often the opportunity came only after a proven career in the cloister: John Stoke, who

[17] *Amundsham*, 2:198, 346-47; *Registrum Whethamstede*, 2:298; Oxford, Bod. MS Laud Misc. 697 fols 26r-27v.

graduated B. Theol. in c. 1430, had begun his studies some fifteen years after full admission to St Albans.[18]

Those St Albans monks who did reach Oxford seem to have enjoyed more wide-ranging, longer and more distinguished academic careers than those from many other communities. Most remained at Gloucester College to complete at least a bachelor's degree, and of those who did return to St Albans as non-graduates none was in the schools for less than two years. Moreover, a significant proportion of the abbey's students went on to complete the doctorate: in Walsingham's generation no fewer than eight returned to the cloister as doctors in theology and canon law. The evidence also suggests that St Albans monk-students embraced the study of both theology and canon law; whereas in some communities law graduates were almost unknown, between c. 1330 and c. 1470 St Albans produced almost equal numbers of graduates in both disciplines. Most monk-students in Oxford remained within the confines of the monastic college, the focus of all their teaching and learning, but the St Albans scholars seem to have ranged much further in the wider academic community. Both William Binham and Nicholas Radcliffe disputed with *magistri* in the principal theology school at the convent of the Austin friars, apparently enjoying a period of "regency" denied to monk-scholars from many other houses. Simon Southerey and another later graduate Hugh Legat, active in Oxford from c. 1400-c. 1420, both seem to have remained in the university for some time as teachers, Legat perhaps as a teacher of the *ars dictaminis*. The contribution of the St Albans monk-scholars to the intellectual life of the university was still commemorated in the mid-sixteenth century in stained-glass windows in the chapel at Gloucester Hall, the names of both Legat and Whethamstede being recorded.[19]

For all their distinctions within the schools, the impact of the St Albans monk-scholars on learning in the home community should

[18] *Gesta abbatum*, 3:425, 480, 486, 518; *Amundsham*, 1:34, 36, 182, 220; A. B. Emden, *A Biographical Register of the University of Oxford to AD 1500*, 3 vols (Oxford, 1957-59), 2:1252, 1987.

[19] Worcester, Cathedral Chapter Library MS F 65 fols 5r, 20r; BL MS Harley 5398 fol. 130r; Dugdale, *Monasticon*, 4:405.

not be exaggerated. It has already been noted that the office of claustral *lector*, to be filled by a returning graduate, was never established at the abbey. The activities of the university monks were also limited by the tendency of the later abbots to disperse them throughout the St Albans dependencies, as priors, chaplains and other obedientiaries, as a deliberate means of ensuring they would not form a powerful and potentially ungovernable group in the mother-house. Even those who did remain at St Albans tended to be occupied with administrative roles rather than in study; graduates such as Binham and Radcliffe held the onerous office of archdeacon; and many other graduates, including Southerey were frequently employed as the abbot's representative on domestic, capitular or even royal and parliamentary business. In one respect only, perhaps, did the returning graduates bring the influence of the schools directly to bear upon education and scholarship in the cloister; encouraged by the abbots, they did become active preachers in the cloister and the local community. Five sermons, in Latin and English, survive from the fourteenth and fifteenth centuries; two in Latin, intended for the cloister, address matters of monastic discipline, two in English expound the dangers of heresy in the parishes, and another in Latin, meant perhaps for a mixed religious and lay audience, celebrates the role of the abbey itself as a spiritual centre.[20]

As a whole, however, the monk-graduates seem to have remained ambivalent about their academic experiences; many did identify themselves by their academic titles and write and speak of the interests of "Mother Oxford", but at the same time they also made a clear distinction between their university studies and their monastic vocation and continued to invoke the traditional monastic *dictum*, as expressed by Walsingham, that "the wisdom of the world

[20] Oxford, Bod. MS Laud Misc. 706 fols 144r-51v; 153r-56r; Worcester, Cathedral Chapter Library MS F 10 fols 8r-13v; 83rb-84va. For further evidence of monk scholars preaching see also *Amundsham*, 1:53; *Registrum Whethamstede*, 2:30, 146; Pantin, *Black Monk Chapters*, 2:135, 142.

is foolishness and secular philosophy vanity in the face of God; neither will bring man to full perfection or sanctity".[21]

Perhaps more significant was the impact of universities on the monk-students as individuals, and in particular the introduction the schools offered them into wider scholarly circles in which their intellectual interests might be sustained even after their return to the home community. In the *Gesta* Walsingham implies that Simon Southerey is known as a scholar "throughout the kingdom", and there is evidence to suggest that soon after returning to St Albans from Gloucester College he was drawn into a vigorous circle of like-minded scholars with Oxford connections. In 1382 he attended the Blackfriars council, convened to examine and condemn the work of Wyclif, and in 1392 he also represented his order at an anti-heretical council at Stamford. His role in these councils seems to have brought him to the attention of the circle of Oxford scholars on the fringes of the Ricardian court, including Dr Adam Stocton, an Austin friar renowned for his interest in classical literature, Dr John Eyton, an Austin canon theologian and Dr Thomas Merke, titular bishop of Carlisle, distinguished for his work as a master of *dictamen* and rhetoric. By the time of Richard's deposition, Southerey was in receipt of a royal pension and was an active member of a circle of classical scholars which included Eyton, Richard Courtenay, an Oxford graduate and later bishop of Norwich and John Seward also an Oxford man and a London schoolmaster.[22] It seems it was Southerey's association with these men which drew him towards the studies in rhetoric and poetry for which, according to Walsingham, he had a nationwide reputation. There is evidence to suggest that several other St Albans monks continued to develop

[21] CUL MS Ee 4.20 fols 99v-100r; *Amundsham*, 1:13, 62, 437; 2:240; *Registrum Whethamstede*, 1:109, 130, 360; H. T. Riley, ed., *Thomae Walsingham quondam monachi sancti Albani Historia Anglicana*, Rolls Series 28/1 (London, 1863-64), 1:307, 345 (henceforth *Historia Anglicana*); *Gesta abbatum*, 2:299.

[22] W. W. Shirley, ed., *Fasiculi zizanniorum*, Rolls Series 5 (London, 1858), p. 241; *Gesta abbatum*, 2:279-80; 3:436; *Historia Anglicana*, 1:189-92; Pantin, *Black Monk Chapters*, 3:323; V. H. Galbraith, "John Seward and his Circle: Some London Scholars of the Early Fifteenth Century", *Mediaeval and Renaissance Studies* 1 (1941), 189-215.

their intellectual interests through similar circles. Hugh Legat, who took the B.Theol. at Gloucester College in c. 1415, seems to have been drawn into an extended circle of scholars and graduates while he was still a student at the university; he and his associates exchanged a series of comic, rhetorical letters with each other, letters similar to those which a century later circulated in the circle around the Evesham monk-scholar Robert Joseph. Following his return to St Albans in c. 1420, Legat maintained these scholarly associations; one of his letters was included in an anthology compiled by a senior Oxford theologian in the later 1430s and identified with the note "brother Hugh, our master" (*magistrum nostrum*); the texts of several of his sermons were also included in collections compiled at St Peter's Gloucester and Worcester priory, communities where he was known to have had associates.[23]

The St Albans monks were not only drawn into a wide range of intellectual activities through their own increasingly rigorous training programme, but also through their involvement as teachers themselves in the education of the laity. Walsingham places particular emphasis on the importance of the abbey as a centre of education; in the *Gesta* passage cited above he maintains the monks were responsible for the training of two distinguished bishops and royal clerks, and in another of his treatises also written in the 1390s, *Defensio de prerogatiuis et dignitatibus ordinem monasticum concernentibus*, he claims monasteries exist not only "for the honour of God, but also for the use of the common weal (*ad utilitatem rei publice*) because there young clerks are nurtured, thus to be raised to divers positions in the church or are educated for the government of the state" (*rem publicam*).[24] Walsingham's claims

[23] Legat's letter survives in BL MS Harley 5398 fol. 130r, an Oxford book, BL MS Cotton Julius F vii fols 129r-35r, from Norwich priory and BL MS Royal 10 B ix fols 170r-73r, from Christ Church, Canterbury. His sermons are found in Oxford, Bod. MS Laud Misc. 706 fols 153v-56r and Worcester, Cathedral Chapter Library MS F 10 fols 8r-13v. For Robert Joseph see below pp. 73-85.

[24] BL MS Cotton Claudius E iv fols 322va-31va at 330vb "... et clericuli in eisdem sustentatur et per consequens ad diuersos gradus ecclesie promonentur uel ad regendam rem publicam educantur". See also Pantin, "Some Medieval Treatises", pp. 214-15.

were exaggerated, reflecting his determination to counter Wyclifite denunciations of monastic communities with arguments for their social role. Nonetheless, there is considerable evidence to bear out his view of the monks as energetic teachers in the local community. From the early fourteenth century, the monks seem to have established a school in the abbey almonry offering instruction in Latin grammar to local boys. Similar institutions were established elsewhere and were intended primarily as a means of guaranteeing future recruitment levels. The St Albans school perhaps addressed this need, but there are indications that it did, as Walsingham claimed, serve as a route for the able and ambitious to establish themselves in clerical and secular careers outside the cloister. Thomas de la Mare's register, compiled in the 1380s, includes a large number of letters of introduction and recommendation concerning young men "whom we have had amongst us for some time".[25] The recollections of William Wintershill, de la Mare's chaplain, confirms the impression of the school as a route to secular careers; the abbot, he wrote, "maintained the boys in his chamber, ministered to them and instructed them" and how "afterwards dispersed in various parts of the kingdom they tell of the generosity and holiness of the men of this place".[26] The fourteenth- and fifteenth-century chronicles from the abbey and the conventual *Liber benefactorum* record the names of several *alumni* whose later careers had taken them beyond the monastic precincts; Thomas Fayrman, who died in 1441, had become a merchant of the staple at Calais; the notorious William Gryndcobbe, "educatus, nutritus et exhibitus" at St Albans had later led the townsmen in revolt in 1381; and John Barnet and Thomas Hatfield, also "nurtured in this place", had entered Edward III's court as clerks and had ended their careers as bishops.[27]

There is some evidence to suggest the abbot and convent not only made provision for grammar teaching but also offered

[25] CUL MS Ee 4.20 fols 81r, 85r, 91v, 124r.

[26] Cambridge, Corpus Christi College MS 7 fol. 118rb.

[27] BL MS Cotton Nero D vii fol. 138r; BL MS Cotton Claudius E iv fol. 334r; *Amundsham*, 2:304-5; *Gesta abbatum*, 3:300; *Historia Anglicana*, 1:468-70.

instruction, or at least the opportunities for instruction, in the common law. An inventory of burials within the abbey compiled in the 1440s records the burial of four apprentices-at-law (*iuris Anglie apprenticius*) in the cloister. It seems these were part of a group of young men maintained within the community in the same way as the almonry boys and perhaps centred on the large permanent body of clerks and notaries engaged on conventual business in the abbot's household; one such apprentice, Roger Hussey (not amongst those buried in the cloister), was recorded as living in the abbey in the 1430s and was ordained to minor orders together with two novices. The nature and extent of the legal education these apprentices received remains unclear: two are described as students of "the law of England" which implies the common law, others simply as students "of law". On the face of it, monastic chanceries would not have been the best environment in which to learn the operation of the common law, and it is possible that these students were in fact learning the more practical arts of the notary.[28]

Amidst such diverse intellectual activities leading the monks from cloister, choir and chapter house out into the secular community beyond the precinct walls, it remains difficult to identify a single, dominant cultural tradition. Walsingham's own recollections suggest the most active scholars and writers at late medieval St Albans had been almost entirely overtaken with the concerns of the Oxford schools and the imperative to counter the spread of heresy and irreligion which the writings of Wyclif had initiated. To some extent this impression is borne out in the books and writings which survive from the later fourteenth and fifteenth centuries. Certainly the greater part of the books copied, commissioned or bought by the abbot and convent between 1330 and 1465 were academic texts, most of them theological: even John Whethamstede, who is best remembered for his interest in humanistic writings, compiled and copied more works of scholastic theology than he did literary commentaries or copies of the work of classical authors.[29] Amongst these acquisitions are several which suggest a clear responsiveness to the latest academic trends. A

[28] *Amundsham*, 1:49, 439, 441, 444.

[29] Sharpe, *English Benedictine Libraries*, pp. 555-62, 575-77.

fragmentary list of monks borrowing books at the Lenten *electio* from c. 1430 records a copy of Nicholas of Lyre's postils on the Old and New Testaments which had belonged to a fourteenth-century monk-scholar, Roger Sulthere. Roger had studied at Oxford in the 1360s but seems to have died soon after as his name disappears from the list of the community. He must have acquired his copy of the postils therefore before 1370, at least a decade before the earliest reference to them in any other English monastic book collection.[30] The copies of William Woodford's *De causis condemnationis*, Adam Easton's *Defensorium* and Thomas Netter's *Doctrinale*, attested to in the writings of Nicholas Radcliffe and the book-inventories of Whethamstede also indicate a similar responsiveness to academic debates in the aftermath of Wyclif's condemnation; Woodford and Easton were not read widely outside the universities, and yet the St Albans monks seem to have held multiple copies of their most important treatises.[31]

The condition of the surviving books suggests the monks devoted much of their private reading time to the study of such academic theology. From the distribution of marginal notation it seems for the most part these studies ran parallel to the university theology curriculum; copies of the Lombard's Sentences and the quodlibets attributed to Alexander of Hales are amongst those most heavily glossed, glosses rich in the language and terminology of the schools, such as "nota pro theologia bonum processum" and "secundum Scotum". Similar texts and authors dominate those recorded in the fifteenth-century *electio* list: one borrower was loaned Peter Comestor's *Historia scholastica*, the *Compendium ueritatis theologiae* attributed to Thomas Aquinas, the Lombard's Sentences and also – a taste of contemporary Oxford – Richard of

[30] Sharpe, *English Benedictine Libraries*, pp. 555-62; M. R. James, *Ancient Libraries of Canterbury and Dover* (Cambridge, 1913), pp. 211-15, 498; J. T. Fowler, ed., *Extracts from the Account Rolls of the Abbey of Durham*, 3 vols, Surtees Society (London, 1898-1901), 2:471.

[31] Sharpe, *English Benedictine Libraries*, pp. 563-81; BL MS Cotton Otho B iv fols 12v-16r; California, San Marino, Huntington Library MS HM 27187 esp. fols 33v, 135v, 151v, 163r.

Wetheringsett's *Summa theologie*.[32] Many of the monks' own compositions also reveal the influence of the university's theology faculty. Their Latin and English sermons are rigidly academic in both form and content, each adheres to the structure of three distinctions, each is based around the *sententiae* of academic authors, led by "Aristoteles princeps philosophorum" and each addresses the same central themes, the importance of clerks as mediators of doctrine through preaching, the irreligion of the people and the laxity of the parish clergy, and the evils of Wyclif and the Lollards.[33] Indeed the monks' absorption of the values of the universities' *magistri* seems to have led them, as Walsingham claims in his memoir, to devote much of their writing to the condemnation of Wyclifite heresy and the defence of orthodoxy. Nicholas Radcliffe composed a series of dialogues addressing some of the themes at the heart of the Wyclifite debate including the limits of civil dominion and the legitimacy of religious vows, his discussion drawing on scripture and on the work of recent controversialists such as Richard Fitzralph and the Durham Benedictine Uthred of Boldon. Simon Southerey is also known to have written a number of similar treatises, including a defence of the Eucharist, although none is known to survive. Walsingham himself compiled an apologia for the monastic life, responding to Wyclif and other "detractors and liars of the present time".[34]

In contrast to other comparable communities, such as Christ Church, Canterbury, Durham and Worcester, the St Albans monks' interest in academic texts and topics did not extend to the logical

[32] London, Lambeth Palace Library MS 111 fols 7r, 12v, 43r; Oxford, St John's College MS 130 fol. 139v; Sharpe, *English Benedictine Libraries*, pp. 555-62.

[33] St Albans sermons survive in Oxford, Bod. MS Laud Misc. 706 fols 143r-51v; 153r-56r; Worcester, Cathedral Chapter Library MS F 10 fols 83rb-84va.

[34] BL MS Royal 6 D x fols 1r-277r; Oxford, Bod. MS Bodley 292 fols 220r-410v. For Southerey's work see J. Bale, *Scriptores illustrium maioris Britanniae* (Basle, 1557), p. 456; T. Tanner, *Bibliotheca Britannico-Hibernica* (Oxford, 1747), pp. 682-83; Emden, *Biographical Register*, 3:1734.

and philosophical debates current in the faculty of arts.[35] No recognisable arts texts survive amongst the fourteenth- and fifteenth-century books and none are recorded in the *electio*-list fragment. According to Gerard Langbaine, writing in the seventeenth century, Thomas Walsingham was the author of a treatise on natural philosophy, *Natura est duplex*, but there is no direct attribution in either of the surviving manuscripts, and subject-matter and style are in marked contrast to Walsingham's other works. John Whethamstede records several arts texts, including the work of William Milverley and Walter Burley, in his book inventories, but as with his other books it is unlikely that these entered the main conventual collection.[36] Subjects on the fringes of the formal arts curriculum, in particular the natural sciences, however, do seem to have exercised more interest in the cloister. Several of the older books in the collection which included scientific texts were repaired, rebound and rubricated in the later fourteenth and fifteenth centuries and reassigned to the cupboards in the cloister; in the 1350s an early thirteenth-century anthology, including Themistius' translation of Aristotle's *De celo et mundi*, was glossed and re-paginated for the use of readers. In the same decade an anonymous monk rebound and annotated a similar collection of treatises '*in quaterni*', including the work of Arzachael, which had been purchased from the executors of Richard de Bury, bishop of Durham, and in the early fifteenth century another reader added a scheme of marginal notes to an anthology of astronomical tables copied in the hand of Matthew Paris.[37] The monks' interest in natural sciences, and in particular astronomy, can to some extent be attributed to the work of Abbot Richard of

[35] Dobson, *Durham Priory*, pp. 360-83; James, *Ancient Libraries*, pp. 168-69, 307-34. For arts at Worcester see the manuscript anthologies Worcester, Cathedral Chapter Library MS F 73, MS F 116, MS F 118, MS Q 54.

[36] For *Natura est duplex* see Oxford, Bodl. MS Bodley 676 fols 149v-62r; London, Lambeth Palace Library MS 456 fols 136v-41r. For Whethamstede's books see Sharpe, *English Benedictine Libraries*, pp. 138-39, 662.

[37] Oxford, Bodl. MS Selden Supra 24 fols 13r, 42v, 65r; Dublin, Trinity College MS 444 esp. fols 9v-10r; Oxford, Bodl. MS Ashmole 304 fols 31v-32r, 41r-v, 52v, 56r.

Wallingford (1326-1334), who had a distinguished career in the Oxford arts faculty before he entered the cloister and who continued his astronomical studies at St Albans. Much of the scientific work done at St Albans in the later fourteenth and fifteenth centuries was based on the abbey's copies of Richard's treatises, including his horological manual, the *Tractatus Albionis*. It is clear, however, that these later generations also continued to follow the lead of the Oxford science masters: a revision of Wallingford's *Albion*, compiled in c. 1400 by John Westwyk, a monk of the St Albans cell at Tynemouth, was based on an earlier revision of the text made in Oxford by a Franciscan scholar Dr Simon Tunstede.[38]

It would be misleading, however, to suggest that academic interests suffocated older and more distinctively monastic traditions of thought in the St Albans cloister. There is considerable evidence to suggest that the monks remained committed to older, non-academic forms of scriptural studies. The fragmentary *electio* list reveals a clear preference for the work of early exegetes, including Hrabanus Maurus, Peter Comestor and Smaragdus, whose commentary on Philippians which appears in the list, was almost unknown in later medieval England. The monks' continuing taste for the more old-fashioned commentaries also seems to have led them to repair and restore their most decayed books for renewed service in the cloister: according to Walsingham a copy of Comestor's *Historia scholastica* given by a twelfth-century abbot was "renewed" (*innouauit*) under de la Mare's supervision. Several other of the earliest books also show signs of repair and restructuring for use in claustral studies; one early thirteenth-century copy of Augustine's commentary on the Psalms belonging to the cell at Hatfield Peverell was even given a whole new scheme of glosses in c. 1400.[39]

[38] For Wallingford see J. D. North, *Richard of Wallingford*, 3 vols (Oxford, 1976), 2:1-21, 271-78. For Westwyk's treatise see Oxford, Bod. MS Laud Misc. 657 fols 1r-78r esp. 1v; for another annotated version of the *Tractatus Albionis* see Oxford, Corpus Christi College MS 144 fols 44r-122v.

[39] Sharpe, *English Benedictine Libraries*, pp. 555-63; BL MS Cotton Nero D vii fol. 49v; BL MS Royal 5 C xi fols 7r, 8r, 10v, 12v, 185v.

It is clear that the monks also continued to make extensive use of liturgical texts in their private studies. Each borrower recorded in the *electio* list had been loaned at least one liturgical book and none of them were juniors who might be expected to borrow such texts in order to learn them. The continuing use of liturgical texts in claustral studies caused some of the oldest manuscripts to be re-commissioned: several late twelfth- and early thirteenth-century psalters were given new rubrics and running-heads and reassigned from the book-room to the cloister cupboards. A thirteenth- and early fourteenth-century anthology of Marian devotions from the cell at Hertford was filled with later medieval marginal notes, many of them prayers and pious observations which suggest the book was used in claustral meditations. The monks' preoccupation with liturgy is further demonstrated by the comprehensive glosses added to the mid fourteenth-century copy of John of Tynemouth's *Sanctilogium*. Glosses were inserted following almost every individual *uitae* detailing the votive antiphons and feasts which related to the saint in question.[40]

In addition to their academic and more conventionally monastic interests, the readers, scholars and writers at late medieval St Albans also drew on wider intellectual currents. In particular, the books of the late fourteenth and early fifteenth centuries reveal a renewed interest in the study of classical literature, comparable in some respects to the new classicism which had emerged in continental Europe. Several of the abbey's oldest books containing the work of classical authors were repaired and reassigned to the cloister cupboards, including much-treasured early twelfth-century copies of Pliny's *Natural History* and Terence's *Comedies*. The monks also acquired a significant number of new copies of the work of classical authors: Hugh Legat bought early twelfth-century copies of Cicero's *De inuentione* and pseudo-Cicero's *Rhetorica ad herennnium* for use in the cloister, a manuscript which also included

[40] Sharpe, *English Benedictine Libraries*, pp. 555-63; London, Lambeth Palace Library MS 420 fols 91r, 94v, 95r, 97v; BL MS Cotton Tiberius E vi fols 10v, 23r, 35v, 65r.

a single leaf scribbled with extracts from Seneca's *Troas*.[41] The monks' interest in these books seems to reflect a new fascination both with classical history and mythography and with the sources for ancient grammatical and rhetorical teachings. Marginal notes in the Pliny and the Terence highlight details of the pagan gods and the deeds of Roman emperors; Legat's Cicero texts are surrounded with notes on rhetorical *flores* together with paradigms from classical authors.[42] These interests are further reflected in the monks' own compositions. John Whethamstede is well-known for his literary scholarship, but what is less familiar is the number of other monks with classical interests who were also active at St Albans.[43] As Walsingham claims in the passage cited above, Simon Southerey was a distinguished literary scholar. Nothing survives of his writings except a handful of verses, but in the *Somnium*, a long, allegorical treatise by the London grammar-master John Seward, he is described fulsomely as "an intimate of the Muses" and a latter-day "Quintilian ... Prince of the Apollonian stronghold".[44] Thomas Walsingham himself was a classical scholar of considerable stature. His compilations, which include a commentary on Ovid's *Metamorphoses*, the *Archana deorum*, histories of Alexander and the Trojan war and a genealogy of the pagan gods, reflect extensive knowledge of a wide range of ancient authors and reveal a strikingly unmonastic willingness to consider classical fables on their own terms.[45] Hugh Legat was also the author of commentaries on

[41] Oxford, New College MS 274 (Pliny); Oxford, Bod. MS Auct 2. 3. 9 (Terence); Sharpe, *English Benedictine Libraries*, pp. 553, 555-62; BL MS Harley 2624 (Legat's Cicero); Oxford, Bod. MS Auct inf. 1. 1 (Dionysius de Burgo Sancti Sepulchro); Oxford, Bod. MS Rawlinson D 358 fols 102r-4v .1

[42] Oxford, New College MS 274 fols 66r "Nota de laude Iulii Cesaris", 86v "nota miraculum de Delphiis"; Oxford, Bod. MS Auct. 2. 3. 9. fols 10r, 23r, 41v; BL MS Harley 2624 fol. 3r.

[43] For Whethamstede's classical interests see R. Weiss, *Humanism in England in the Fifteenth Century* (Oxford, 1941), pp. 30-38; D. R. Howlett, "Studies in the Works of John Whethamstede" (unpublished D.Phil. dissertation, University of Oxford, 1975).

[44] Edinburgh, University Library MS 136 fols 42v-68r.

[45] For Walsingham's classical compilations see BL MS Harley 2693 fols 121r-68v (*Prohemia poetarum*); Oxford, St John's College MS 124 (*Archana*

Boethius' *Consolation of Philosophy* and the pseudo-classical *Architrenius* and composed letters and sermons in which he cultivated a florid Ciceronian style.[46]

This classicism seems to have been born out of the monks' connections with a variety of learned communities. Southerey, Legat and Whethamstede had come under the influence of dictaminal masters active in Oxford in the early years of the fifteenth century, whose work promoted the imitation of classical rhetorical and metrical styles. At the same time, these and other St Albans monks also made contact with European classical scholars through their attendance at ecclesiastical councils and the curia. There are some indications, especially noticeable in Walsingham's work, that the monks' taste for classical history and mythography was part of a revival passing through many religious communities in the late fourteenth and early fifteenth centuries: Walsingham himself does seem to have been in touch with like-minded scholars in houses such as Bury St Edmunds and the convent of Austin friars at York.[47]

The books and writings which survive from late medieval St Albans can be seen therefore to reveal not the remnants of a moribund cultural tradition but the working papers of a diverse range of vigorous scholars and teachers. As Thomas Walsingham had suggested in his own memoir, the late medieval community was notable for its active university-trained *magistri*, who studied and wrote on academic theology in the cloister and expounded their views, especially their hostility to Wyclifism, amongst the laity. The

deorum); Oxford, Bod. MS Douce 299 (*Historia Alexandri magni*); Oxford, Bod. MS Rawlinson B 214 fols 1r-110v (*Dites ditatus*).

[46] Emden, *Biographical Register*, 2:1125-26. For copies of his writings see BL MS Harley 5398 fols 130r-31v; Oxford, Bod. MS Digby 64 fols 108r-20v; Oxford, Bod. MS Laud Misc. 706 fols 153v-56r; Worcester, Cathedral Chapter Library MS F 10 fols 8r-13v.

[47] For the dictaminal masters and their influence see *Formularies which bear upon the history of Oxford*, ed. H. E. Salter, H. G. Richardson and W. A. Pantin, Oxford Historical Society, new ser. 5 (Oxford, 1942); M. Camargo, *Medieval Rhetorics of Prose Composition* (Binghampton, 1995). For classical scholars at ecclesiastical councils, see E. F. Jacob, *Essays in the Conciliar Epoch* (Manchester, 1943), pp. 76-78; Galbraith, "John Seward", pp. 189ı-215.

evidence also indicates that the monks' involvement in education extended further, to include the teaching of grammar and even the common law within the abbey precincts. There is nothing to suggest that academic studies undermined the monks' commitment to other forms of learning; the books reveal a continuing interest in traditional monastic culture, which emphasised scriptural and liturgical meditations as acts of devotion fundamental to claustral life and a responsiveness to the new classicism which emerged in secular learned communities in the first decades of the fifteenth century. It would be misleading to draw too broad a conclusion from this picture, to maintain that the same combination of monastic, academic and other cultural trends flourished throughout English Benedictine cloisters in the later middle ages: in its size, wealth and learned traditions St Albans was an exceptional house. But this brief examination of its late medieval books could nonetheless be taken as an indication of what might be revealed elsewhere when historians discard the old assumptions of decadence and decline and return to the evidence of what the monks themselves read, thought and wrote.

Dissolution and De-Conversion: Institutional Change and Individual Response in the 1530s

Peter Cunich

The dissolution of the monasteries was once considered to be an integral component of that series of religious and political changes which are collectively known as the English Reformation. In more recent times, however, historians of Tudor England have had to revise this interpretation as it has become increasingly clear that the dissolution owed more to Henry VIII's lust for money and land than it did to a desire for reforming the monasteries of his kingdom.[1] The old view that the monasteries were dissolved because they harboured "manifest sin, vicious, carnal, and abominable living" has therefore been superseded by an explanation which emphasises financial rather than religious and political considerations. Consequently the dissolution is today seen primarily as a "revolution in landownership"; an unprecedented example of "naked expropriation" by the crown.[2] This shift in interpretation has had the effect of diverting the attention of historians away from the issues of monastic discipline which characterised earlier debates and has refocused discussion upon the financial ends of the whole

[1] Youings, *Dissolution*, p. 13.

[2] Youings, *Dissolution*, pp. 155, 15; Richard Rex, *Henry VIII and the English Reformation* (London, 1993), p. 58; A. G. Dickens, *The English Reformation*, 2nd edn (London, 1989), pp. 167-68.

dissolution process. In the last forty years, therefore, debate over the moral state of the monasteries has given way to a series of increasingly sophisticated analyses of the financial gains made by the crown from the dissolution. These studies have provided us with a detailed understanding of the process by which ex-monastic lands were acquired, administered and alienated by the crown,[3] but they have also unintentionally done much to stifle research into the purely religious aspects of the dissolution.

The dissolution of the monasteries was not simply a massive financial transaction between the crown and the hundreds of religious communities in the kingdom. While large numbers of religious were probably induced to sign the deeds of surrender for "base and material motives", it would be unwise to ascribe these motivations to the whole monastic population of England.[4] There can be no doubt that the religious who faced the prospect of being turned out of their monasteries were concerned with the personal financial consequences of suppression, but there were other issues to be considered when these men and women were making decisions about their futures. The religious life involved more than just financial security, and a large proportion of the monastic population must have been as exercised by spiritual concerns as they were by the meaner temporal considerations of life outside the cloister. We should remember that despite the instances of monastic venality, greed, lasciviousness, disobedience and indolence which historians have discovered in the visitation records of the 1520s and 1530s, there is a large volume of evidence indicating that on the eve of the dissolution a sizeable portion of the English regulars were at the very least observing their religious vows, and a number of houses were providing edifying examples of strict observance.[5] It is a very simplistic view of monasticism which presumes that a

[3] The majority of these studies have taken the form of doctoral dissertations. For a list of these works see my unpublished Ph.D. dissertation, "The administration and alienation of ex-monastic lands by the crown, 1536-47" (Cambridge, 1990), pp. 135-41.

[4] Youings, *Dissolution*, pp. 20, 62-63.

[5] For example, see Knowles, *Religious Orders*, 3:87-107, 206-7, 212-15, 222-29.

concern for physical security is incompatible with an observant lifestyle. In between the two extremes of venality and sanctity there was a large body of men and women whose attitudes to the religious life tended towards moderation. In order to understand better the predicament in which these moderate religious found themselves at the dissolution, we should be seeking to identify the widest possible spectrum of observance within the eight hundred or so religious houses in the kingdom.

We search in vain for accounts of what it meant spiritually and psychologically for individual monks and nuns to be expelled from a way of life which many had chosen as adolescents. Consequently, it is not possible to say with any certitude exactly what these monks and nuns felt when they were expelled from their cloisters. One approach which might be taken in attempting to gain a fuller appreciation of their spiritual and emotional turmoil is to consider their responses to the threat of suppression in the context of their profession as religious. Because religious profession had always been recognised as a form of conversion,[6] the dissolution of monastic communities may be considered as the beginning of a process of de-conversion for individual religious. This deconversion involved more than just a simple physical return to the world beyond the monastery gate. The quest for monastic conversion upon which the novice embarked when entering the religious life was a path which promised to lead him towards the heights of perfection.[7] The daily life of a religious was controlled by the rule of the order, and a lifetime of close observance of that rule was meant to internalise the ideals of the monastic life and thereby accomplish an ever more complete conversion of mind and soul within the individual monk or nun. Even those monks and nuns who jumped at the opportunity to leave their walled precincts and throw off the

[6] Knowles, *Religious Orders*, 3:461.

[7] Rule of St Benedict, 73.2 (*RB 1980*, p. 295). I use the term *monastic* conversion here in a general sense. By it I mean the process of religious formation by which all regulars (monks, nuns, canons regular and friars) were distinguished from the laity and the secular clergy. I am not therefore referring exclusively to monks and nuns, which a narrower use of the term would imply.

yoke of religious profession cannot have been entirely untouched by their many years within the cloister.

Monastic conversion began during the year of novitiate which all candidates for the religious life were expected to serve. At the end of this year of preparation the novice was professed by taking perpetual vows. These vows differed from order to order, but in late medieval England nearly all monks, nuns and canons regular took the vows of stability, conversion of life, and obedience.[8] For St Benedict, whose rule was the model for the majority of religious in Tudor England, the cardinal principle of the monastic life was obedience to the abbot, but a novice's vows to live within a particular monastic community for life, and to strive for a continuing conversion of lifestyle were the secondary means by which the professed religious would ascend towards spiritual union with Christ.[9] It is important to emphasise that members of most religious orders in sixteenth-century England, with the notable exception of the mendicant friars, took these three vows at profession. They are rather different from the three vows commonly ascribed to monks and nuns today – poverty, chastity and obedience – vows which in the later middle ages were taken principally by mendicant friars. There has been some confusion in the past as to what vows a religious made upon profession in the early sixteenth century,[10] and this confusion has in turn led to some misinterpretations of what was expected of the newly professed as an observant religious. Observance at its most basic meant simply a fidelity to profession vows and the rule. It did not guarantee that a religious would scale the heights of spiritual perfection. Only a few

[8] Rule of St Benedict, 58.17 (*RB 1980*, p. 269), in which "conversion of life" is rendered as "fidelity to monastic life".

[9] C. H. Lawrence, *Medieval Monasticism: Forms of Religious Life in Western Europe in the Middle Ages*, 2nd edn (London, 1989), p. 29.

[10] For example, David Knowles does not deal with the question of vows and profession in *Religious Orders*, vol. 3; and Donald Logan, in his recent book on monastic apostasy, *Runaway Religious in Medieval England, c. 1240-1540* (Cambridge, 1996), p. 19, incorrectly implies that the vows taken by all medieval religious were those of "obedience, chastity and poverty", although his example on p. 20 actually uses the correct formula of "stability, moral conversion and obedience".

people in each generation achieved true monastic sanctity; the majority of monks and nuns led unremarkable lives which were punctuated by the usual human failings and achievements.

Monastic conversion also relied on factors other than the rule and the profession vows taken by the novice. The personal characteristics of a religious determined the strength of an individual's commitment to the precepts of the monastic life. Some temperaments flourished under the strict monastic regime while others were less suited for it. The period of time since profession may also have had an impact on the degree to which a religious was observant. Younger monks and nuns were perhaps more likely to question authority and give in to human temptation but the more mature members of monastic communities were probably less prone to such failings; this is where the spiritual temperature of a community would either support or fail the individual monk or nun in critical periods of formation. The spiritual temperature of a house in turn depended on a large number of factors ranging from local geographical conditions to the special traditions and customs of particular orders and monasteries. The sex of a religious was another factor which played an important role in formation. Men and women experienced very different types of monastic conversion, men normally being destined for the priesthood and a more active participation in the life of the secular church. Women were destined for perpetual seclusion and gender roles which were in keeping with societal norms at the time. It must also be remembered that there were hierarchies within monastic orders reflecting the division of work within the cloister between the choir and the lay religious. The formation of a religious was also to a large extent determined by the type of work which he or she was destined to do within the community. A life of monastic observance for an abbot or senior obedientiary was very different from that of a novice or a lay brother.

Given the range of factors both spiritual and temporal which determined monastic formation it is not possible to understand monastic conversion in Tudor England by using a simplistic model which likens religious formation to a standardised vocational training programme which all regulars undertook. Even though the basic precepts of the religious life were similar for all, the existence in England of seventeen orders and more than eight hundred religious houses meant that there were enormous variations in the process of monastic formation. While it is true that monastic conversion entailed a great deal of shared and common experience, it must also be recognised that the end product could be as varied as the characters of each of the ten thousand or so professed religious.

It is surprising how little consideration has been given to this notion in previous assessments of English monasticism on the eve of the dissolution. Most commentators are satisfied to present a rather less than sophisticated analysis of monastic observance in Tudor England. Professor Knowles was content to identify three basic groups of religious. At one extreme there were those who were "seriously striving after perfection", while at the other there were those who were totally "unworthy" of their monastic profession. In between there was a "large body of respectable men and women who were contented and useful members of the society to which they belonged".[11] Although this rather imprecise view of the range of religious fervour within English monasteries seems to have been accepted by most commentators for the last forty years, there are others who have realised that the situation was far more complex.[12] Generalisations do not help us to understand the multiplicity of ways in which individual religious responded to the challenges of the dissolution. If we accept that there were many varieties of monastic conversion, then we must also recognise that when the dissolution came in the 1530s there were bound to be many different responses to the pressures generated by the deconversion process. A more comprehensive analysis of both the conversion and deconversion processes must therefore be attempted if we are to reach a deeper understanding of what the dissolution meant to the individual monk or nun in the 1530s and 1540s.

The process of monastic deconversion which took place as a result of the dissolution is thus a very complex matter which requires sophisticated analysis. It is not, however, the intention of

[11] Knowles, *Religious Orders*, 3:403.

[12] Joyce Youings is one of the few commentators who draws attention to the fact that the religious houses varied enormously "as to material comfort and disciplinary standards": Youings, *Dissolution*, p. 23.

this essay to offer a comprehensive treatment of the subject. Rather, an attempt will be made to reassess some of the evidence relating to the ways in which the vows taken by religious predisposed them to certain types of action at the time of the dissolution. In discussing these issues I hope to suggest some new directions for further investigation. It is not possible here to examine all the English religious orders, so this study has been limited to the strictly monastic orders – Benedictine, Cluniac, Cistercian and Carthusian.[13] These orders shared much in common in terms of religious profession and the type of religious formation which took place after profession, even though there were distinct differences between them. They were not exclusively male, but the female religious, numbering approximately 1,300 nuns, tended to have very different experiences of conversion and deconversion compared to their male counterparts. This essay will therefore concentrate only on the male religious. Limited though this survey is, the 181 monastic houses and approximately 3,000 monks and lay brothers in the sample represent around forty per cent of the population of male religious in England during the 1530s.[14] Apart from their numerical significance, the monks offer the added advantage of having left behind them a relatively large archive of evidence in comparison with the non-monastic orders and the nuns. Even so, there are still very wide gaps in our understanding of the impact of the dissolution on individual monks and much of what follows remains speculative at this stage.

In considering the impact of the dissolution on professed monks our starting point will be the premise that all fully professed monks were to a greater or lesser extent changed by their experience of monastic conversion in the years leading up to the dissolution.

[13] I have not included the Bridgettine monks and lay brothers in this study.

[14] This survey includes 79 independent houses and 60 cells and dependent priories of Benedictine monks (approx. 1,650 monks); 16 houses of Cluniacs (200 monks); 77 houses of Cistercians (1,050 monks and *conversi*); and 9 houses of Carthusians (150 monks and 40 or more *conversi*). These numbers are drawn from work in progress on a biographical register of religious at the time of the dissolution.

The vows which they made at profession and the life which they led thereafter in their cloisters made them essentially different from other members of the clergy. The dissolution of a monastic community was a *terminus a quo* which was characterised by the dispensation of monks from certain vows which were specific to the monastic (but not the clerical) state. The practical impact of the dissolution on monastic communities was immediate. Without a locus for the community, without a head to whom obedience was owed, and denied a lifestyle in the cloister which made conversion of life in its narrowly defined monastic sense possible, the monastic life for English monks became untenable. There are no recorded instances of male monastic communities attempting to continue their regular life after the dissolution of their houses as there are for female monastic communities.[15] Their immediate concern not surprisingly appears to have been the problem of reintegration into secular society.

Most discussions of the ways in which ex-religious adjusted to the secular world have tended to focus on the provision of pensions and the post-dissolution career prospects of the former monks.[16] For some monks the dissolution no doubt offered a heaven-sent opportunity for release from religious vows together with chances for social and economic advancement which the cloister had denied them. But there were probably very few of these monks left in their cloisters by the late 1530s. Most of them had already grasped at the opportunity to be dispensed from their vows in the mid-1530s.[17] For the majority of monks who had decided to continue in the religious life, the sudden trauma of having to compete for employment in a clerical job market swamped by ex-religious must have been extreme. They undoubtedly found it extremely difficult to adjust to

[15] See Marilyn Oliva's essay in this volume, pp. 87-104.

[16] See especially Hodgett, "Unpensioned Ex-religious", pp. 195-202.

[17] A total of 123 monks are recorded as having been granted dispensations to leave the monastic life in the period 1534-38, but there were probably many others who did not follow this formal path in leaving the monastic life; see D. S. Chambers, *Faculty Office Registers 1534-1549: A Calendar of the first two Registers of the Archbishop of Canterbury's Faculty Office* (Oxford, 1966), especially pp. xlv-xlvi.

the demands of the secular world, especially those who had spent longer periods as religious. A rough survey of the monastic orders in the late 1530s (after the dissolution of the smaller houses) indicates that by the end of the decade between eighty and ninety per cent of English and Welsh monks had been professed for more than ten years, and in some houses the figure was even higher.[18] In fact, a surprisingly large proportion of monks had been in religion for more than twenty years and it was not uncommon to find men who had been professed for thirty or more years. It is not therefore surprising to find that many monks were determined to remain inside their cloisters until the last possible moment, presumably hoping for a stay of execution.

That large numbers of monks wished to continue in the religious life is evident from the way in which the more powerful houses were able to fend off suppression until the second half of 1539. This was achieved despite the increasing pressure applied by the king's commissioners on abbots and priors from mid-1538, and the passing of the second dissolution Act in May 1539. This resistance to suppression is particularly noticeable among houses of Benedictine and Carthusian monks. The majority of houses in these two orders did not surrender until the last year of the decade (see table). In fact, for nearly eighty per cent of Benedictine monks (1,287) and approximately two-thirds of the Carthusians (124), conventual life carried on until the middle of 1539. Such resistance to suppression contrasts sharply with the commonly-held view that the monastic houses rushed to surrender as soon as it was in their financial interests to do so.

The Carthusians were especially tenacious in their efforts to continue leading their rigorous and enclosed lifestyle. Despite the constant badgering they received from Henry VIII's dissolution commissioners, seven out of nine houses survived until 1539. The inducements for the Carthusians to surrender were compelling. The order had played a prominent role in resisting the religious changes

[18] This figure has been drawn from research currently under way which aims at constructing a *Monastic Database for sixteenth-century England and Wales*, for which see the World Wide Web home page at <http://www.hku.hk/history/cunich/monast1.html>.

of the mid-1530s and, by the end of 1537, no less than eight Carthusian monks had been executed for refusing to submit to Henry VIII's changes in religion and another nine had perished in the Fleet prison.[19] Relatively generous pensions were awarded to the remaining monks of the London Charterhouse who surrendered in 1537 and to the monks of Axholme who surrendered in the wake of Archbishop Cranmer's efforts to dislodge the prior in 1538, but such rewards were shunned by the remainder of the Carthusian houses. The Witham, Beauvale and Hull Charterhouses had already purchased exemptions from suppression by paying large fines to the crown in 1536 and 1537. The monks of Witham were plunged into extreme poverty in the second half of 1537 as a consequence of raising money to save their house. Forced to sell all their plate, cattle and timber, they also had to borrow money in order to raise sufficient cash to pay their fine.[20] The prior of Hinton was equally determined to preserve his convent, refusing to surrender the house unless directly ordered to do so by the king.[21] Carthusian resistance to voluntary surrender continued throughout 1539 and even resulted in the prior of Mount Grace being incarcerated for a time at York Castle in early 1540.[22] For Carthusian monks, then, the vow of stability was taken very seriously, even in the dying days of English monasticism.

The responses of the Benedictine and Cistercian monks to the challenges of the dissolution were much more varied than their more austere confreres in the Carthusian order. There were several notable examples of heroic resistance to Henry VIII's programme of

[19] For a fuller account of the Carthusian resistance see Knowles, *Religious Orders*, 3:222-40. William Horne was the only monk to survive his imprisonment in the Fleet but was later executed at Tyburn on 4 August 11540.

[20] *Letters and Papers, Henry VIII*, 12(1):744, 882, 883. In September 1538 it was alleged that the procurator of the house, Thurstan Hickman, was "no good husband" in managing the finances of the priory and that it would soon be in ruins if he were allowed to continue in office, but it seems likely that Witham never fully recovered from the fine imposed on it in 1537 (*ibid.*, 13(2):Appendix, 39).

[21] *Letters and Papers, Henry VIII*, 14(1):145; Hinton was finally surrendered on 31 March 1539 (*ibid.*, 14(1):637).

[22] *Letters and Papers, Henry VIII*, 14(2):749, 750; 15:125.

forced suppressions, but the general picture painted of Benedictine and Cistercian monks as they faced an uncertain future has been one of venality and self-interest. It has been argued that these monks were simply trying to prolong the good life of cloistered indolence for as long as possible.[23] This accusation rings true in the case of Thomas Goldwell, prior of Canterbury cathedral priory. His frantic efforts to save the priory from dissolution and his mounting desperation about his own future career provide clear evidence of a man who had become accustomed to his privileged life as the head of a wealthy monastic house. In spite of a long record of incompetence in the administration of his monastery and the marked antipathy towards him of both Cranmer and Cromwell as the 1530s progressed, Goldwell pleaded that he be appointed as dean of the new secular cathedral chapter which was to replace the old monastic establishment. At sixty-two years of age, a professed monk since 1493, and prior for the last twenty-two years, Goldwell felt that he would not be able to adjust to life as a secular priest without some position of rank in the ecclesiastical hierarchy of the kingdom.[24] For this reason, Goldwell has been described as self-serving in his pathetic efforts to gain preferment after the dissolution of his house.[25] No doubt there is much truth in this assessment. Goldwell was certainly no saint, but his desperation is understandable given that he had been professed as a sixteen-year-old boy and for forty-six years had lived as a Benedictine monk.

Goldwell was not alone among the heads of Benedictine houses in asking that his house be saved from suppression. The superiors of Pipewell, Evesham, Great Malvern, Cerne and York St Mary's all requested that their monasteries be spared in the twelve months immediately prior to the last wave of surrenders.[26] These

[23] Youings, *Dissolution*, pp. 20, 62-63.

[24] *Letters and Papers, Henry VIII*, 15:254 (24 February 1540) is Goldwell's pleading letter to Cromwell.

[25] Barrie Dobson, "The Monks of Canterbury in the Later Middle Ages, 1220-1540", in *A History of Canterbury Cathedral*, ed. Patrick Collinson, Nigel Ramsay and Margaret Sparks (Oxford, 1995), p. 152.

[26] *Letters and Papers, Henry VIII*, 13(2):1036; 13(1):1330; 13(2):866, 1092; 14 (2):490.

monastic prelates were all ultimately disappointed in their efforts as indeed Goldwell was in his bid for the deanship of Canterbury cathedral. But the majority of the former cathedral priors were appointed to the deaneries of the refounded cathedrals and some eventually became bishops. Indeed, the majority of Benedictine abbots and priors did very well for themselves in terms of pension provisions and ecclesiastical preferment. However, this does not mean that all heads of Benedictine houses were infected by greed at the prospect of life outside the cloister. Richard Whiting of Glastonbury governed his house in a manner which was universally admired by his contemporaries,[27] while Abbot Melford of Bury St Edmunds (1513-39) and Prior Whitehead of Durham (1520-40) seem to have been exemplary heads of these important Benedictine establishments.[28] It is not possible to judge with any accuracy the general level of observance in these great Benedictine monasteries on the eve of the dissolution, but apart from a few well-documented examples of immorality in certain houses, there is little in the records to suggest that laxity and incontinence set the tone of Benedictine monasticism in the 1530s.

In terms of physical comfort, the Benedictine abbeys were probably the best appointed monasteries in the land. Miss Harvey's recent study of Westminster abbey leaves little doubt that the monks of this royal foundation lived a life of relative comfort and ease despite the demands of their monastic profession.[29] Such levels of comfort were not, however, universal among the Benedictine houses. At Battle abbey, for example, the "household stuff and vestments" were described as "the poorest ever seen in any abbey or priory", and at Abingdon, not even the abbot's lodgings were in a satisfactory condition for lay habitation according to the report of the commissioners.[30] A comfortable lifestyle was therefore not necessarily the reason why so many Benedictine monks chose to remain in religion in 1537 and 1538.

[27] Knowles, *Religious Orders*, 3:379-80.

[28] *Letters and Papers, Henry VIII*, 9:772; 10:183.

[29] Harvey, *Living and Dying*, especially her concluding comments on pp. 210-12.

[30] *Letters and Papers, Henry VIII*, 13(1):1084, 332.

Nor were the Benedictines free from persecution by the crown. While they did not suffer the same degree of rough persuasion which was meted out to the Carthusians, monks from a number of Benedictine houses fell foul of the authorities. Six monks of Bardney were executed after the Lincolnshire rising of 1536 and there were several other examples of Benedictines who were imprisoned on suspicion of treason between 1536 and 1540.[31] The warning implicit in these scattered incidents was reinforced in very blunt terms with the imprisonment and execution of the abbots of Glastonbury, Reading and Colchester together with two of the most senior monks of Glastonbury towards the end of 1539. From this moment the great Benedictine abbeys tumbled one after another in quick succession, but even as late as 9 November 1539 the abbot of York St Mary's was asking that Cromwell might spare his house from suppression.[32] Likewise, the abbot of Evesham and the prior of Great Malvern had urged that their monasteries might be put to some other use. These houses were doomed to fall in the last wave of suppressions, but several other dissolved Benedictine monasteries were refounded as communities of secular priests in the early 1540s.[33] While this tenacity may be attributed to an inability to change with the times, it is just as reasonable to presume that the members of some Benedictine communities simply wished to continue living according to the vows which they had made at profession and the rule which regulated their daily lives.

[31] These monks included William Ashwell, third prior of St Albans (*Letters and Papers, Henry VIII*, 11:354; August 1536); a monk of Abingdon "too weak to send up" to London (*ibid.*, 13(2):275; February 1538); Ambrose Caster of Peterborough (*ibid.*, 13(1):1159; June 1538); Robert Anthony, sub-cellarer of Canterbury cathedral priory (*ibid.*, 13(2):24 and 97; August 1538); Thomas Powell, cantor of Bath abbey (*ibid.*, 13(2):532; October 1538); William Jerome, cellarer of Winchcombe (*ibid.*, 14(1):55; January 1539); and Roger London, monk of Reading (*ibid.*, 14(2):554; November 1539).

[32] *Letters and Papers, Henry VIII*, 14(2):490.

[33] Burton-on-Trent became a secular college in 1540 while Westminster, Canterbury, Rochester, Winchester, Gloucester, Worcester, Peterborough, Ely, Chester and Durham were refounded as cathedral chapters. Norwich cathedral priory had already been converted into a secular cathedral chapter in 15 38.

The situation was rather different for the houses of the Cistercian and Cluniac orders. By the end of 1538, seventy per cent of all Cistercians (742 monks) and Cluniacs (137 monks) had either been evicted or had left their monasteries by choice (see table). This at first appears to be damning evidence of a decline in monastic fervour, but a closer examination of the sequence of events which led to the surrender of so many Cistercian and Cluniac houses in 1537 and 1538 casts a degree of doubt over the strength of such assertions. As in the case of the Carthusians, the crown had sent out very strong warning signals to these two orders in the earlier stages of the dissolution. Ten Cistercian monks were executed in March 1537 in the wake of the Pilgrimage of Grace and another three in the summer of 1538. In addition to these executions, two monks of Furness were imprisoned at Lancaster and a monk of Roche was held at York on suspicion of treason in the same year.[34] The abbot of Vale Royal was forced to surrender his house in 1539 after having been threatened with trumped up charges.[35] Likewise, the prior and two monks of the Cluniac house of Lenton were executed for treason early in 1538.[36] In many of these cases the punishment of monks was not directly related to the dissolution process but such exemplary punishments must certainly have been recognised by other monastic communities as potent warnings of what might be expected in the future should they resist royal policies.

Another significant problem for the Cistercians was that more than half of their houses were valued at below the £200 per annum threshold and so were marked for suppression in 1536. Slightly less than half of the Cluniac houses found themselves in a similar position.[37] Although ten of the Cistercian houses were successful in their attempts to purchase exemptions from suppression in 1536, this was not enough to prevent many of the wealthier houses from surrendering voluntarily from the middle of 1537. The attainder of important monasteries such as Jervaulx, Kirkstead, Whalley and

[34] *Letters and Papers, Henry VIII*, 12(1):841 (3).

[35] *Letters and Papers, Henry VIII*, 13(2):314.

[36] *Letters and Papers, Henry VIII*, 13(1):787.

[37] Forty-one of the seventy-seven Cistercian houses were valued at less than £200 per annum, and seven out of the sixteen Cluniac houses.

Sawley in 1537, followed by Woburn in 1538, convinced many other Cistercian convents that resistance to the crown was futile. Twenty-one of the greater Cistercian houses therefore fell during 1537 and 1538. The first voluntary surrender was that of Furness abbey, one of the largest Cistercian houses, on 5 April 1537, probably as a result of the involvement of a number of its monks in the Pilgrimage of Grace.[38] A similar loss of nerve appears to have undermined Cluniac resistance to the dissolution commissioners. Lewes priory, the largest and most important Cluniac house in England, surrendered on 16 November 1537, closely followed by its daughter house at Castle Acre. Then, on the first day of the new year, the great London priory of Bermondsey, headed by a commendatory prior who had been appointed by Thomas Cromwell, was dissolved. After this, Cluniac resistance crumbled. Even so, the prior and convent of the Cluniac house of Montacute were among the most obstinate of the monks in the west country when it came to resisting the king's commissioners. The resistance of Montacute is one of the more prominent examples of a monastic community which proves to be an exception to the opinion that whole orders of religious collapsed under pressure from the crown. The story of Bermondsey is also instructive. How many communities of otherwise observant monks were disbanded due to the actions of abbots and priors who had been appointed for that very task by Cromwell?[39] Would it have been possible for rank-and-file monks to stand against their superiors when told that they were expected to sign away their monasteries to the crown? Perhaps we expect too much of these unworldly men, trained from an early age to obey their superiors, when we ask why they did not resist royal pressure for longer than they did.

[38] *Letters and Papers, Henry VIII*, 12(2):652, 841; its income was £805 per annum.

[39] This was certainly the case for a number of the great Benedictine monasteries. At Worcester cathedral priory, Henry Holbeach was elected at Cromwell's order in 1536 and surrendered the house four years later. See Joan Greatrex, *Biographical Register of the English Cathedral Priories of the Province of Canterbury c. 1066-1540* (Oxford, 1997), pp. 761, 824.

That the Cistercian and Cluniac resistance to suppression was weaker than that of the Benedictine and Carthusian monks should not come as any surprise. In general the Cistercian and Cluniac monks were less well-educated, their houses were neither as wealthy nor as influential politically, and living conditions must have been less comfortable for the rank-and-file of monks. Poverty did not, however, necessarily induce these communities to surrender in return for crown pensions. The monastic buildings at Revesby and Thame, for example, were described by the commissioners as being much decayed and nearly ruinous in 1538, but the monks stayed on until the last year of the dissolution. They were not alone. At the beginning of 1539, nineteen Cistercian and four Cluniac houses were still standing in defiance of Cromwell's unceasing efforts to induce voluntary surrenders. What is surprising, considering the events of the previous two years, is that so many of these monasteries had been able to sustain their resistance to the crown as it attempted to effect a wholesale sequestration of the monastic estates.

This interpretation gives an impression which is at odds with the traditional assertions that the monastic orders caved in very quickly when pressure was applied by the crown in the late 1530s. The pressure was certainly extreme in the case of the Carthusians and the Cistercians, but the fact still remains that approximately sixty per cent of the entire population of English monks resisted surrender until the final wave of dissolutions in 1539-40. This perhaps indicates a far greater attachment to monastic vows than has been allowed by previous commentators. Further evidence of the lingering power of the vow of stability over former monks is to be found in the way in which they tended to settle within a short distance of their former monasteries. Even twenty-five years after the dissolution, the majority of surviving monk-pensioners from the Benedictine houses of Evesham, Pershore, Shrewsbury and Peterborough were still living in the vicinity of their former monastic homes.[40] Likewise, the refoundation of Carthusian and Benedictine monasteries at Sheen and Westminster during the reign

[40] This information is derived from the returns of Elizabeth I's commissioners; for which see PRO, LR5/23.

of Queen Mary, a full fifteen years after the dissolution, attests to the survival of a strong commitment to the religious life among monks of certain houses and orders.

This commitment to the religious life has been underestimated in previous assessments of English monasticism on the eve of the dissolution. It is true that the English state was remarkably successful in sweeping away the entire institution of monasticism in a relatively short space of time, but the responses of individual religious to this institutional change are now seen to be as varied as the monastic houses and the monks who filled them. While some monks were quick to leave the cloister for financial or other considerations, the majority stayed on until the end. Although the traumas they experienced have left very little trace in the formal records of the period, it is possible to understand at least in part the situation in which the ex-religious found themselves. More research needs to be done before we can begin to talk about patterns in the responses of individual religious to the dissolution, but perhaps one conclusion can be drawn from this limited survey of English monasticism in the sixteenth century. Like all large institutions, the English monasteries have developed a corporate image in the minds of historians, and there is a tendency to imagine that individual members of large corporations all think and feel the same way in certain situations. In reality, the English monasteries were home to many thousands of individuals who, when faced with crisis, made personal responses and chose different courses of action. This must be the starting place for a more sophisticated analysis of the dissolution and its impact upon the ex-religious.

Monastic Houses Dissolved in the Three Stages of the Dissolution[41]

	1536-37		1538		1539-40		Total	
	houses	monks	houses	monks	houses	monks	houses	monks
Benedictines	21	151	13	226	45	1,287	79	1,664
Cluniacs	9	84	3	53	4	60	16	197
Cistercians	37	447	21	295	19	302	77	1,044
Carthusians	1	40	1	11	7	124	9	175
Totals	74	732	38	585	75	1,773	181	3,080

[41] These figures are abstracted from data being collected for a *Monastic Database for sixteenth-century England and Wales*; see World Wide Web page, <http://www.hku.hk/history/cunich/monast1.html>.

Westwood, a Rural English Nunnery with its Local and French Connections

Margaret Goodrich

> In a vast and solitary wood ... was bylded a Nunnery for religious weomen who, retyred from the world, weare devoted to God.[1]

Thus wrote Thomas Habington, the Worcestershire antiquarian, of Westwood priory eighty years after its end. He was exaggerating a little; the wood may have been vast but it was not especially solitary as it lay within a mile of Droitwich, known to medieval people as Wych and renowned for its salt production. In some ways the nunnery was like any other of medieval England, built in the countryside, housing a small community of women and endowed with just enough land and financial dues for them to follow their dutiful life but on the edge of poverty. But of course, each nunnery was different and Westwood had some interesting distinctive features. Useful comparisons can also be made with other local nunneries: Whiston outside Worcester, often known as White Ladies and Cookhill priory on the Warwickshire border.

The circumstances of Westwood's founding were not unusual. Eustachia de Say, a noblewoman and her son Osbert FitzHugh established the house early in Henry II's reign. The exact date is uncertain but may well have been about 1158 since a royal

[1] T. Habington, *A Survey of Worcestershire*, ed. J. Amphlett, 2 vols (Worcester, 1893), 2:311.

confirmation of their lost founding charter can probably be dated to April 1158; and Bishop Alfred of Worcester, who approved another grant, was in office 1158-1160. As late as Edward IV's reign the Crown regularly reconfirmed the original charter but it is only referred to as of Henry II.[2] The founders were of the new French aristocracy and so were able to give the priory a reasonable endowment including the site at Westwood with land around it, land at adjacent Crutch, a salt pit in Wych and, at Cotheridge several miles away, the church and its dues. At the same time Osbert FitzHugh granted, with the consent of Bishop Alfred, another nearby church to the nuns, that of St Augustine's, Dodderhill.[3]

This last gift, however, soon brought the nuns into a tiresome dispute which must have marred the first years of their existence. The monks of Worcester cathedral priory maintained that St Augustine's church was theirs, that Osbert FitzRichard had appropriated it to them and that the gift had been confirmed by Bishop Samson of Worcester (1096-1112) and his two successors.[4] But the nuns contested that they also had been given the church with episcopal confirmation and they were not going to give it up easily. Westwood was a new foundation, needing all the resources available of money and kind, as the nuns built and equipped their convent and learned the management of their farms. The wrangle went on for twenty years, the nuns' case backed by a powerful, though distant supporter; for amongst their dispositions for the nunnery, Eustachia de Say and her son had committed it to the order of Fontevrault.

Thus the abbess of Fontevrault took up Westwood's case but the women finally had to give way to the men. Adelburga, third abbess of Fontevrault, wrote to Bishop Roger of Worcester, not giving up her order's claim, rather expressing surprise that the monks of Worcester should presume to dispute it. Yet to prevent further contention, she would allow the dispute to go to arbitration and abide

[2] *Calendar of the Patent Rolls preserved in the Public Record Office* (London, 1901-) (1476-1489), p. 69. Henceforth this is cited as *CPR*, with the medieval dates of the volume in brackets.

[3] R. Darlington, ed., *Cartulary of Worcester Cathedral Priory* (London, 1968), p. 88.

[4] *VCH Worcester*, 3:276.

by that decision.[5] It all sounds very modern. One of the arbitrators was FitzHugh himself and in 1178, although the monks won Dodderhill church, the Westwood nuns, in compensation (probably at Osbert FitzHugh's insistence), gained all the land in Clerehall and all tithes of their lands in the parish of Dodderhill. That is, the lands of Westwood, Clerehall and Crutch with the accompanying burial rights and obventions, all local and all most useful.[6]

With the intervention of Fontrevault, Worcester cathedral priory had been unable to subdue Westwood as it might have done some less well placed house. The Fontevrault connection was a prestigious one and the mother abbey near the Loire was a favourite of Henry II and his family. Robert d'Arbrissel had founded the order in 1101-2 and from its beginning it enjoyed royal approval. The kings of France and England gave generously for the building of the great abbey church, and Eleanor of Aquitaine, Henry II's formidable queen, particularly favoured the foundation. She spent much time there with the nuns as her life wore on and at death was buried in the church, where her husband, Henry, and son Richard, Coeur de Lion, already lay. The heart of King John also lies at Fontevrault, though his body is entombed before the high altar at Worcester. The abbesses, nearly half of whom claimed royal descent, answered directly to the Pope in spiritual matters, and in temporal affairs to the French king's royal council.

Robert d'Arbrissel had founded his order to house both men and women, that is as a double order. Indeed, within the enclosure at Fontevrault five different houses developed: the nuns' house with the great abbey church, the monks' house, and also St Lazare a leper hospital, St Benoît for the sick and elderly, and Ste Madeleine a house for repentant women. The abbess ruled supremely over all five, with both spiritual and temporal authority. In England there were only three daughter houses, Westwood, Nuneaton and Amesbury. This background must have given the nuns at Westwood considerable confidence. They could argue the toss with the prior and bishop in

[5] Darlington, *Cartulary*, p. 88.

[6] Birmingham Central Library, Archives Division, BCA Hampton MSS, 281 (henceforth Hampton MSS).

Worcester and expected reasonable compensation for surrendering Dodderhill church.

However, good connections did not make the Westwood house wealthy. Although a series of charters and the *Valor Ecclesiasticus* record widespread land holding, none of it was particularly rich and most only in small parcels.[7] Around the priory the nuns held the small manors of Westwood, Clerehall and Crutch and within a ten mile radius they leased out land and held land directly in many places. Their furthest holdings lay in distant Gloucestershire, in Cold Aston and Little Aston villages.[8] Locally, the nuns took the dues from three mills and had been given some useful privileges. These were typical of the time. Jocelin de Wich, for example, allowed them toll-free passage for hay and corn wagons over his Brerhulle bridge from hay-making until Michaelmas, extended for their wood carts until All Saints' tide.[9] In 1280, the lay subsidy roll assessed the manorial lands with other holdings, at 56s. The spiritualities which would have included the tithes of Cotheridge and Westwood, Clerehall and Crutch came to £2. By 1535, according to the *Valor Ecclesiasticus,* the value of the nuns' estates had risen but still stood at only £75 clear which made them wealthier than many other small houses. In comparison, Cookhill priory was valued at £34 in 1535 and Whiston at £53.[10]

Unlike the other Worcestershire nunneries, a considerable number of Westwood's primary documents have survived. While evidence for Cookhill and White Ladies can only be found second hand from entries in the bishops' registers, the Worcester priory records and those of central government, Westwood presents a different picture. At the dissolution Henry VIII granted John Pakington the monastic site and lands and his descendants lived at Westwood until the 1890s. Fortunately the family realised the value of the medieval documents and today they are deposited in the Worcester Record Office and Birmingham Central Library as part of

[7] *Valor Ecclesiasticus*, 3:276.

[8] *VCH Worcester*, 2:148.

[9] Dugdale, *Monasticon*, 6(2):1009.

[10] *Valor Ecclesiasticus*, 3:27 (Westwood), 263 (Cookhill), 230 (Whiston).

the Pakington and Hampton papers.[11] The Worcester records include charters, manorial court and account rolls. At Birmingham the archive is extensive: there are over a hundred documents, all relating to the priory and its possessions. Some are fragmentary or scarcely legible but much is there to be studied. The deposit includes leases, quit-claims, grants of land and property as well as letters of protection and account rolls. These last include the accounts of several bailiffs, a prior, a chaplain and, unusually, that of a surveyor of a "bullary of salt water", as well as the prioresses' accounts. In date they range from 1178 to just beyond the dissolution, and provide a precious resource for the study of monastic economy, medieval agriculture and the history of Westwood priory.

The account rolls indicate that cash flow must often have been a problem for the prioress and her bailiff. They largely depended on rents for the priory's money income and if these fell behind, as has been found in other nunneries they frequently did, the priory would have had problems. The account rolls show payments to craftsmen and other employees such as shepherds and cowherds, and the charters record the nuns often paying for the repair of their conventual buildings or for the shelters and barns on their farms. On the receipt side, for grants of land there were one off cash payments or smaller sums paid once or twice a year. For example, when Ralph Hacket gave the convent salt-producing land in Wych, they accepted it by paying one silver mark.[12] Fortunately, as a Fontevrault house, the nuns were not subject to the local episcopal jurisdiction so they did not suffer expenses such as visitation fees.

An unusual feature of Westwood priory's economy is the part salt played in grants to the house or annual dues it owed. This is not surprising with its proximity to Wych. Some of the Westwood charters reflect the nearby industry. In their founding deed Eustachia de Say and her son, as we have seen, bestowed on the nuns a *salinarium* (a brine boiling place) at Wych, and later amongst other salt grants, Alured Laverun of Wych presented them with an annual two shillings rent from a *puteum* (a brine pit), the money to be spent

[11] Hereford and Worcester Record Office, BA 3835 (henceforth HWRO); Hampton MSS.

[12] Dugdale, *Monasticon*, 6(2):1008.

on tallow lights for the convent.[13] Perhaps he had visited the priory one winter evening and was shocked by the paucity of the lighting arrangements. Another donor, Osbert Bende, bestowed on the priory land in Wych, with two and a half *helflingis salsae* (measures of salt). But they in return owed six *panelios* of salt (probably small baskets) each year; the nuns received salt but they also had to give it, often as an annual due.[14]

For anyone studying the medieval salt industry the records of Westwood priory provide a valuable resource. Many different salt making terms and measures appear and the place of salt in grants and property agreements is clearly displayed. The account roll (c. 1400) mentioned earlier of John Woodeward, "surveyor of a bullary of salt water belonging to the prioress and convent of Westwood", would make a good starting place.[15]

From the records, by means of the account rolls, it is possible to look at the priory before and after the Black Death and assess a little of the impact of the plague. Most scholars agree that early in the troubled fourteenth century there was already a marked agricultural change. Farming prosperity was declining well before the plague struck in 1348-49. The deteriorating weather and an unprecedented growth in population were significant factors. The situation was at its worst between 1315 and 1322 when torrential rain and severe droughts brought desperate years. Crops were ruined, grain prices soared, a murrain hit the sheep and cattle and the malnourished poor, always living at subsistence level, died. As the population declined, prices steadied by the 1330s and 1340s because of the drop in demand. Such was the situation before the Black Death hit Worcestershire in late 1348; the resulting mortality which ranged from 20 per cent to 40 per cent, was bound to hasten change.

Wages rose with the scarcity of labour. In 1337 a number of Westwood manor workers earned only 1d a day, including the thatcher and the carpenter.[16] But by 1393 the carpenter's wage had

[13] Dugdale, *Monasticon*, 6(2):1007.
[14] Dugdale, *Monasticon*, 6(2):1007.
[15] Hampton MSS, 319.
[16] *Ibid.*, 308.

more than doubled to 14d a week and a sawyer earned the same.[17] Commodity and animal prices, however, remained stable. In 1337, wax for the church candles was bought at 6d-7d a pound; in 1393 it was the same price. Animal prices are more difficult to compare as beasts varied in quality, size and age but Westwood manor bought two oxen in 1337 for 21 shillings and paid less, 16 shillings and 18 shillings, for the equivalent in 1393. These may have been inferior specimens for another single ox cost 15s 6d in the same year. An account roll for four months in 1350 reflects immediate results of the plague.[18] Although five oxen at nine shillings each show slight change in price from 1337, the wages of John Walsh, ploughman, at Crutch had soared. He earned 18s 4d in twenty weeks, 11 pence a week, compared with his five pence or six pence before the plague. More difficult to categorise is the cost of the prioress' "palefrey" which seems expensive at 38 shillings but an understandable extravagance after the stresses of the plague.

Although only the prioress and convent are named in most of the account rolls, Westwood was undoubtedly a double house. This, of course, derived from the Fontevrault model. Priors are mentioned from 1239 when Nicholas the prior joined with the prioress, Annis, and the convent in a leasing agreement with Henry of Wych.[19] Eight different priors are named through the years and only one remains nameless. They mostly appear joined with the prioress and convent in charters of various kinds. For example, a lease of August 1319 begins "Beatrice, prioress of Westwood and Richard, prior of the same place, with the consent of the whole convent".[20] On one occasion canons are mentioned as well when the Worcester *Sede Vacante* register records that the "prior, prioress and canons of Westwood" granted William Was of Shrawley half a measure of "good pure and well winnowed corn every week for life" (1352).[21] But otherwise the

[17] *Ibid.*, 316.
[18] *Ibid.*, 309.
[19] *Ibid.*, 86.
[20] *Ibid.*, 53.
[21] J. W. Bund, ed., *The Register of the Diocese of Worcester during the Vacancy of the See, usually called Registrum Sede Vacante 1301-1435* (Worcester, 1893-97), p. 201 (henceforth *Reg. Sede Vacante*).

brothers or canons remain unknown figures although there was probably a group of them at Westwood for many years.

The last prior to be recorded is William in 1371, and so it appears that for about 150 years, perhaps longer, male religious shared the Westwood enclosure. Whether they lived in a separate house with their own church or lived in a part of the priory and shared the nuns' church is not known. Unfortunately at Westwood the site of the nunnery building is totally lost, thus there is no relevant archaeological evidence which might indicate where the brothers lived. Most likely, following the Fontevrault arrangement, the men lived separately as Augustinian canons while the nuns kept the Benedictine rule. Abbess Marie de Bretagne of Fontevrault in a letter to the Pope of 1459 described this as the situation at the mother house and adds that she was supreme over all. In England, no doubt, the arrangement was the same. At Nuneaton and Amesbury priors and canons appear and, as at Westwood, fade from the scene: at Amesbury after 1403 and at Nuneaton after 1424. In Amesbury they had been present since its foundation in 1177 and at Nuneaton they are recorded from the fourteenth century but may well have been present many years before.

The prior of Westwood appears to have worked with the prioress in managing the priory land and he probably was more likely than she to ride out with the bailiff to visit the distant holdings. Indeed, there is the extant account roll of Robert de Southerey, prior, made for the priory lands from May to September 1350.[22] In the middle ages nunneries must often have been disadvantaged in land management. The prioress if a typical gentlewoman, would be unlikely to have known much about day by day farming, leaving her dependent on her steward or bailiff who might not always be scrupulously honest. In fact, in 1385, William Monk, once both chaplain and bailiff at Westwood, lay in the Fleet prison for not rendering his account to the prioress.[23] It would also be difficult to chase up rents from distant tenants from the seclusion of the priory, although prioresses were allowed to ride out from the enclosure, and there are even references to nuns in other houses who helped to

[22] Hampton MSS, 309.

[23] *CPR* (1385-89), p. 27.

gather in the harvest. But generally, as in secular life, men would have managed the land and the male employees, and women the domestic affairs. Apart from dealing with the estates, the constant presence of a few men must have given the Westwood nuns a sense of security. Hopefully the prior and brothers provided some protection against aggressive beggars from neighbouring Wych or from preying outlaws in the nearby Feckenham forest.

One prior however, may have been an embarrassment. In 1316, the patent rolls record complaints against Richard "le priour" and Geoffrey his brother who had trespassed on neighbouring land and carried away goods.[24] Regrettably we do not know how such a passing scandal was resolved. One task which a better behaved prior took on for the prioress and probably welcomed as a change from the monastic round, was performed by Prior Robert de Southerey who travelled to Fontevrault to attend the order's General Chapter in 1344. Accompanied by Prior John of Nuneaton he had first to obtain a royal licence to travel since these were the opening years of the Hundred Years War. The licence demanded that the two men were to set out from Dover, and that before they went they were to swear not to reveal the king's secrets to the enemy and to warn him of anything plotted in France against him.[25] Even if this was routine to seasoned wartime travellers, it was diverting for those used to the quiet religious life.

This royal permission to travel to France in wartime seems to indicate the special standing Fontevrault held with the kings of England. The house at Westwood never seems to have been treated as an alien priory. In 1374, when the prior of Worcester drew up his list of alien priories as required by the Crown, Westwood was not on it.[26] It never suffered as others did from its foreign loyalty. In fact it was often excused central taxation and purveyances because of its poverty, along with other small indigent houses. As late as 1405, letters of protection exempted the nuns from a demanding purveyance

[24] *CPR* (1313-17), p. 499.

[25] *Calendar of the Close Rolls preserved in the Public Record Office* (London, 1902-), vol. dated 1343-46, p. 383.

[26] *Reg. Sede Vacante*, p. 307.

of Henry IV,[27] and there are several incidences of their being excused both royal and papal taxes.[28] Although Westwood's first loyalty was to Fontevrault, when the nuns were in contact with local authority they were usually dealt with sympathetically. For example, in 1301, the prior of Worcester instructed a commissary not to take the tithes due to his priory from the nuns' churches because of their poverty.[29]

At Westwood there is no hint of the depredations which other alien priories suffered. It does not appear that Henry V penalised the priory in any way in 1414 when he closed down the remaining alien houses. Perhaps, although there is no record, the prioress and nuns had taken denizen status and renounced the long allegiance to France. Their sister priories of Amesbury and Nuneaton did so, and such an action may be connected with the disappearance of the male element in the three houses.

If the Westwood nuns took denizen status, it is clear they had not done so before 1384, for in that year they became embroiled in an election incident which presumably originated from their Fontevrault loyalty. It was the time of the Great Schism and, following the example of other French dignitaries, the abbess of Fontevrault supported the schismatic Avignonese pope, Clement VII. Isabella de Gros, prioress at Westwood since 1365, did likewise, following the lead of the mother abbess. However, when Isabella died in 1384, the pope at Rome, Urban VI, moved quickly to assert his authority as the English church had given its allegiance to him rather than to his rival. Urban instructed the prior of Worcester to supervise the next election of the prioress of Westwood to secure a woman loyal to Rome as the new head. The nuns chose Edith de Benacre but she was not happy with the post; perhaps she also secretly favoured the Avignonese pope as she resigned shortly afterwards. The sub-prioress, Marie de Acton, took her place, elected by the nuns *una voce et uno spiritu* and Walter the prior of Worcester confirmed the choice and issued all the necessary documents for her installation. Pope Urban considered that the abbess of Fontevrault had forfeited her right to authorise the Westwood election, thus did the ripples of the Schism reach as far as

[27] Hampton MSS, 306.

[28] *CPR* (1292-1301), pp. 97, 264.

[29] *Reg. Sede Vacante*, p. 62.

a small Worcestershire priory. Documents for Marie's election and subsequent elections of Eleanor Porter (1393) and of Isabella Russell (1405) are all to be found in Nash's *Collections* and describe the house as of Fontevrault but the ascription seems to disappear after that time.[30]

The election documents of 1384 and 1405 include useful lists of names of the electing nuns. A further list is that of the nuns professed in 1337.[31] A look at these names and those of the known prioresses can give us some idea of the sort of people the nuns were and the families from which they came. Thomas Habington remarks that "the nunrie of Westwood [was] a place where unto the chiefest gentlewomen of these parts retired themselves from the vanities of this world ...".[32] He may again be exaggerating yet several of the nuns appear to be of good families of local origin. Apart from Marie de Acton, the fourteenth-century prioress, four other nuns and the last prioress are named as Acton. Acton lies only two or so miles from Westwood, an extensive area of good farm land as was probably the case 600 years ago. Whether the surname Acton means the six nuns all came from one land-owning family originating there, or whether they were just from that village, we cannot know. Eleanor Porter, who appears as proctor in the 1384 election, could also have been a very local recruit. A mill close by on the river Salwarpe has long been known as Porter's mill and she may well have come from that mill owning family. We can place Edith Hornyolde, an electing nun in both 1384 and 1405, much more certainly. The Hornyolds are still one of Worcestershire's Roman Catholic families, the unusual name being easily identifiable. Other nuns too seem to have come from not far afield: Elizabeth Norton, Alicia de Feckenham, Alicia de Pershore, Johanna de Egebaston all bear local place names, while Isabella and Agnes Cassy must be related to Sir Thomas Cassy, lord of nearby Hadzor.

[30] T. R. Nash, *Collections for the History of Worcestershire*, 2 vols (London, 1781-82), 1:353-57 where he prints thirteen documents concerning the three elections from Worcester Cathedral Library MS A.5 (Liber Albus) fols 282, 424, 425.

[31] HWRO BA 2648/2, Register of Bishop Hemenhale, fol. 12.

[32] Habington, *Worcestershire*, 2:311.

It seems that Westwood was well known in the area, hence the local recruits; but it was not a prestigious enough house to attract novices from far afield or from very wealthy families. One nun, Isabella Russell, could have come from a more powerful background than the others: her contemporary, Sir John Russell of Strensham, was an important supporter of Richard II. Yet the fact that he left money to the monks of the cathedral priory and to the White Ladies in Worcester but left none to Westwood, casts doubt on any relationship. However, her election as prioress in 1405 may still denote a more commanding background than some of her sister nuns.

Some evidence remains that the founders, as was common practice, had reserved the right of presenting a girl to the convent. In the mid-thirteenth century William de Stuteville, husband of Eustachia de Say's great-granddaughter, is known to have given up this inherited right of presenting *unam monialem*, although he generously renewed all the family's grants to the priory.[33] Another mode of entry to the community was used by Reginald de Bray.[34] He gave his daughter, Amabilia, to the priory along with substantial nearby land, property and rents, which sounds like a dowry although the Benedictine rule officially prohibited this. Could it be Amabilia whose coffin was found centuries later in a pond in Westwood park? Peter Prattinton, writing in the early nineteenth century, described how the inscription, by then much eroded, appeared to read in part, "(L)E CORS D ... MABLE ...".[35] Mable could be a part of Amabilia's name.

There are two other points worth considering about the Westwood nuns. One is the size of the house. It appears to have been the largest of the three Worcestershire nunneries even excluding the male element. Knowles and Hadcock give J. C. Russell's figure of 20 nuns at Westwood's dissolution which the latter incorrectly dates as 1539.[36] However, their figure for 1381 of fourteen nuns seems

[33] Dugdale, *Monasticon*, 6(2):1006.

[34] Dugdale, *Monasticon*, 6(2):1005.

[35] HWRO BA 10509, Prattinton Collection.

[36] D. Knowles and R. N. Hadcock, *Medieval Religious Houses, England and Wales* (London, 1971), pp. 104-5 (Westwood), 273 (Cookhill), 277 (Whiston).

acceptable as that number of nuns took part in the election of Marie de Acton three years later. Comparable figures in Knowles and Hadcock are seven for Cookhill in 1381 and for Whiston nine. Earlier in the century as might be expected, before the Black Death, the Westwood numbers were higher. When Bishop Hemenhale of Worcester came to the priory in 1337 he received the professions of eighteen candidates.[37] They were almost certainly not all newcomers to the community; some had probably been in the house for several years and, though considered tacitly professed, had waited long for their formal profession. All the same, eighteen professions indicates a house of some size; interestingly, this visit of Hemenhale appears to be the only time the local bishop came to the house. Perhaps he had some fellow feeling for the Westwood nuns as previously he had been a monk at Worcester cathedral priory, only six or so miles away. The last figure we have is for the twelve electors in 1405.[38] No numbers survive for the dissolution, apart from J. C. Russell's, not even a pension list for the nuns; only the prioress' pension is recorded.

Another interesting point which derives from the three lists of nuns' names is the apparent longevity of some of them. This belies the idea that most medieval people died young. For instance, the name Isabella Cassy appears in all three lists: she was professed in 1337, so was probably born about 1320 and is named in 1384 and again in 1405. By then she must have been 84 or 85 years old, a hardy survivor of the stresses of the fourteenth century. Another nun, Eleanor Acton, another survivor of the Black Death, appears on the first two lists which would make her about 64 years old in 1384. At the White Ladies in Worcester the picture is similar; existing election lists there again show nuns of 60 to 80 years old.[39] Perhaps the measured monastic round, demanding but not too demanding, and a simple diet, could make for a long life once the body and mind settled into a monastic *stabilitas*.

[37] HWRO BA 2648/2, Register of Bishop Hemenhale, fol. 12.

[38] Nash, *Collections*, p. 357, from Worcester Liber Albus, fol. 425.

[39] M. Goodrich, "The White Ladies of Worcester", *Transactions of the Worcestershire Archaeological Society*, 3rd ser. 14 (1994), 129-47.

Little is known of Westwood priory's end apart from the official sources. In the *Valor Ecclesiasticus* the commissioners valued the priory and all its assets at £75, thus it was doomed for the first round of closure.[40] The local landowner and royal official, John Pakington was quick to seize his chance. He wrote straightaway to Thomas Cromwell asking for the priory of Westwood in farm as he had no pasture for his horses and good steeds were essential, as "I am now in the king's service in north Wales to my great charge".[41] By the next year, 1537, the farm of Westwood was his, although he seems to have felt this not sufficient reward with only a meagre salary of 50 marks for his "painful" office in Wales.[42] Joyce or Jocosa Acton may well have already left with any remaining nuns, probably all returning to their families. Her last steward was one Thomas Acton and a Robert Acton, armiger, who had been one of the *Valor* commissioners, gained some of the priory lands shortly after its closure.[43] This is an interesting coincidence of names which asks the question whether there was an attempt to keep some former monastic land in the family. Here Joyce Acton could have continued to live with some of her former nuns as a quiet secular household. This happened elsewhere but we have no evidence for it at Westwood. A similar conjunction of names appears at the White Ladies. Whatever happened, Joyce Acton had a pension of £10 a year, higher than the prioresses at Cookhill or Whiston, another indication of a larger and better provided house.[44] She lived on until late 1564 when in her will she directed that:

> I, Joyce Acton, sometime prioress of Westwode ... give and bequethe to all hallows church Xs to by a Bible ... .[45]

Clearly Joyce Acton knew what was now religiously correct. It was officially no longer acceptable to leave money for candles or for a Mass for the soul. Instead a Bible had the proper Protestant

[40] *Valor Ecclesiasticus*, 3:276.

[41] *Letters and Papers, Henry VIII*, 10:155.

[42] *Letters and Papers, Henry VIII*, 11(2):275.

[43] *Letters and Papers, Henry VIII*, 13(1):487.

[44] *Letters and Papers, Henry VIII*, 13(1):576. See also below pp. 100-2.

[45] HWRO BA 3590/1, *Will Register*, 6(2), fol. 222.

emphasis. Had she herself accepted the new faith? It would be interesting to know.

John Pakington and his successors set to work to build a splendid mansion on their new estate at Westwood. Tradition maintains that John had such respect for the nuns and their good works that he avoided building on the monastic remains. His great house still stands but the exact nunnery site remains uncertain, although a few worked stones and at least one stone coffin, besides the one referred to above, have been found. Westwood priory's unusual interest lies in its connection with the local salt industry and with distant Fontevrault and, as well, in its recently traced, substantial archive which promises much for monastic studies.

John Lydgate, Monk of Bury St Edmunds, as Spiritual Director

Nicholas Heale

We know that John Lydgate entered the novitiate of the abbey at Bury St Edmunds in Suffolk in the mid-1380s, as he informs us himself, at the age of fifteen;[1] we know that he progressed through the various stages of profession and ordination culminating in his being priested in 1397; and we know that he died half a century and almost 150,000 lines of verse later, in 1449. But whether or not he lived out those intervening years as a good and holy monk, or as a rather worldly monk, or even as a rather glamorous member of sophisticated court society, no two people seem quite able to agree.[2] His verse, the bulk of which translates ancient mythology into

[1] "The Testament of Dan John Lydgate", lines 610, 670 in *The Minor Poems of John Lydgate*, ed. H. N. MacCracken, vol. 1, Early English Text Society (henceforth EETS) es 107 (London, 1911; repr. Oxford, 1962), pp. 352, 354. This volume will be cited hereafter as *Minor Poems I*.

[2] Among the major studies of his work, the most important are: W. F. Schirmer, *John Lydgate: A Study in the Culture of the Fifteenth Century* (London, 1961); A. Renoir, *The Poetry of John Lydgate* (London, 1967); D. Pearsall, *John Lydgate* (London, 1970). Pearsall sees Lydgate as a late expression of medieval culture; Schirmer and Renoir see him as a channel for secular renaissance learning, one, in particular as a political theorist, the other as an early humanist. All interpret him as a poet who happened to be a monk: in contrast I myself see him primarily as a monk, although clearly one with contemporary and fashionable interests.

English, qualifies him to stand as a reasonably distinguished man of letters, and as one of the most important of Chaucer's successors. But it is also rooted in and conditioned by the culture of the cloister which in Bury St Edmunds had been ravaged during the Peasants' Revolt in 1381, but which was also experiencing a significant programme of renewal during the very time when Lydgate underwent his novitiate.[3] The materials which were available to Lydgate in the monastic library at Bury, which was one of the finest in the country, emerge later as sources and models for his poetry.[4] Tracing some of these sources in Lydgate's vernacular moral and especially religious verse encourages the interpretation of at least some of that verse as a specific aid to the religious and devotional life of its readers; and there is some evidence in manuscript copies of his work which gives an indication of who was likely to read it and in what context. By examining all these threads of evidence it becomes plausible, and indeed necessary, to interpret Lydgate's work as a specific response to his own religious life, and as an

[3] The traumas of the Peasants' Revolt are summarised in Pearsall, *John Lydgate*, which includes a chapter on the monastic background; I have myself surveyed the renewal movements at Bury in the late fourteenth century in "Religious and Intellectual Interests at the Abbey of St Edmund at Bury and the Nature of English Benedictinism, c. 1350-1450" (unpublished D.Phil. dissertation, University of Oxford, 1995).

[4] This is true in obvious instances, such as his compilation of an English verse-life of the local patron, St Edmund, where Lydgate follows precisely the Latin *Vita Sancti Edmundi* drawn up within the cloister at Bury a generation before he entered the community (Oxford, Bod. MS Bodley 240, p. 624 et seq). It is also true in more oblique cases, where it is clear that source texts which Lydgate uses have survived from Bury indicating not only that the source in question was available to Lydgate within his own monastery, but even that there were annotations in that copy of the text – unique to that particular manuscript – which he followed in his verse versions in English. This is true, for instance, of annotations about the authenticity of the Immaculate Conception of Mary which appear in a Bury copy of Alexander Neckham's *Marian Commentary on the Song of Songs* (Oxford, Bod. MS Bodley 356, fols 7, 29) and which resurface at the appropriate place in his *Life of Our Lady*. The thorough research of these parallels between source manuscripts from Bury and the finished poems themselves has barely begun, but my impression, having examined both, is that there are many such parallels to be uncovered.

expression of its pastoral value for individuals and groups of laypeople, not only within the monastic confraternity at Bury but also in much wider social circles outside the monastery.[5] It is this process of religious reflection passed on from monk to reader which allows us to begin to think in terms of the spiritual counsel and guidance, albeit at a very basic level, which is at the heart of spiritual direction.

What, then, were the religious focuses of Lydgate's devotional writing? There is a twelfth-century manuscript in the Bodleian Library in Oxford, originally from the monastic library at Bury, which contains an inscription by John Lydgate, marking quite clearly his appropriation of the book for his own use, and including a few of his jottings. The manuscript is full of moralistic sermons and includes a *Liber Penitentialis*, two accounts of the creation of the world, and some proverbs and classical verses.[6] This is not a sophisticated theological textbook, but neither is it devoid of concern for the things of God; rather than any copies of classical or mythological texts, or of the encyclopaedias which have survived from the Bury library, and which also express Lydgate's interests, it is this manuscript which has come down to us containing the mark of Lydgate's ownership. Among his jottings, which are at the back of the book, there is one which says, "Ave Maria, gratia plena, dominus tecum"; another says, "Et veniat super nos misericordia tua domine". It would be a mistake to infer any especially profound religious sentiment from this alone, but this manuscript and those jottings do bring us immediately and directly to the very centre of Lydgate's understanding of things. It is an archetypally monastic manuscript, with a broadly moral focus; and those two verses point us towards a Marian devotion and an awareness of our need for the mercy of God. These themes are at the very centre of Lydgate's

[5] The confraternity at Bury was a group of distinguished lay people admitted as non-monastic friends of the community. It included a large number of the people who are known to have been Lydgate's patrons, and it provided a monastic rather than a secular or courtly focus for exchanges between poet and patrons.

[6] Oxford, Bod. MS Laud Misc. 233. Lydgate's jottings can be found with his signature on the inside back cover.

thought and verse, and they are quite unmistakable in his religious verse.

These things can be obscured by the very nature of the verse which is certainly didactic and formalised, and far from lyrical; it labours its latinate brilliance whilst avoiding totally the affective passion which is what we have tended to condition ourselves to look for and expect in later medieval spirituality. Lydgate's abstracted stiffness jars with the human vulnerability which is often preferred today, and some readers have been more ready to judge his defects as a poet than to seek the signs of his spiritual insight and concern. His contemporaries, however, revered him. It would be extreme revisionism to try to rehabilitate him as a great spiritual luminary, and it is possibly an overstatement even to redefine him as a spiritual director, but these terms do at least provide a point of reference which will enable a more balanced interpretation of his work.

John Lydgate produced about a dozen epic mythological works, which are truly vast, and for which he is best known; but most of his verse is quite short, and most of it is religious. What follows concerns itself with the topics which he considered important in his religious work, the sources which he used, his motives in writing and the audience to which it was addressed. It has been suggested that Lydgate sought to restore a sacred character to religious verse in an age of increasing secularism, and that this accounts for the abstraction and formality of the verse, but this is questionable.[7] John Lydgate, the monk of Bury, immersed in a Latin religious culture, was primarily interested in helping the layfolk of his day with their faith and with their prayers, which is the essence of spiritual direction. There is evidence that people sought this kind of help from the monks: they include Margery Kempe, whose extrovert and outspoken approach to the spiritual life was hardly in keeping with the quieter rhythms of Benedictinism, and who tells us about the encounters which she had with black monks in Canterbury

[7] This is the basic thesis of the chapter on the religious works in Schirmer, *John Lydgate*.

and Norwich, somewhat strained though these were.[8] This paper envisages lay people like her who might have had dealings with John Lydgate and, using his poetry as a source, it looks for the sort of responses and advice they would have received from him.

Lydgate produced religious writing in English for readers of every social station, much of it commissioned by private or institutional patrons from the king down to the inmates of the local hospital for lepers. These works were designed not for public oration, but for domestic devotional use;[9] they were intended to strengthen faith and increase devotion, and as such they form part of that whole wave of vernacular religious writing from the fourteenth and fifteenth centuries which was compiled to inform lay religion. Lydgate's religious verse should be seen as a conscious contribution to that lay spirituality, and as a response to contemporary challenges to orthodoxy. He gently protects his readers against heresy; he helps them to deepen their life of prayer, and especially of liturgical prayer, offering the means to a deeper understanding of what goes on in church. For this reason a great deal of his religious writing is descriptive or explanatory. Sometimes it was composed to operate in a particularly anonymous way, as in the *Prayer to St Leonard* which was pinned up in the chapel of a hospital in Bury, or the *Prayer to St Thomas* made for the shrine at Canterbury;[10] this is also true of the translation of the psalm *De Profundis* which was made to be hung in the nave of the abbey church at Bury to explain its liturgical

[8] S. B. Meech and H. E. Allen eds, *The Book of Margery Kempe*, EETS os 212 (Oxford, 1940), chapters 13, 43. At Canterbury Margery was accused of Lollardy, which, as a form of heresy, accounts for the ill-will felt towards her in the monastery there. Lydgate is not alone among the Benedictines in having made the defence of orthodox faith part of his own programme. See also above pp. 17, 22.

[9] D. Pearsall hints at this in relation to several of Lydgate's religious works in his chapter on the religious poetry in *John Lydgate.*

[10] *Minor Poems I*, p. 136 (especially lines 35-36); p. 143 (The *Envoy* in stanza 15 which also gives some indication of Lydgate's personal motives: "praynge echoon that shal thes seen or rede/ Nat to disdeigne but doo Correccioun"). For clarity I have opted here to adapt the titles of poems into contemporary English, but quotations will be presented in the original dıialect.

use to visitors.[11] There are also references to verses put up in other local churches, such as the parish church at Long Melford, where some of Lydgate's lines accompanied painted images;[12] most of these are short, and all are vernacular works designed to enhance the devotion of the passer-by. They are probably the fifteenth-century equivalent to those cheap tracts which can be found today in churches and monasteries, designed to nurture the simple faith of simple people, and which do genuinely seem to achieve this effect in the religious lives of those who are too modest to seek formal spiritual direction for themselves. Sometimes, however, Lydgate writes for a very specific and very cultivated individual patron such as Isobel, Countess of Warwick, for whom *The Fifteen Joys of Our Lady* was compiled, or Alice, Countess of Suffolk, for whom he wrote *The Virtues of the Mass*,[13] although it is clear that such texts circulated much more widely than their original dedicatees. *The Fifteen Joys of Our Lady* can be interpreted as a modified version of the rosary devotion, taking fifteen episodes from the lives of Christ and of Mary and interspersing them with *Ave Marias*; *The Virtues of the Mass* sets about describing the vestments, the separate components of the liturgy and the ritual of the mass, encouraging quiet prayer, especially at the consecration, when the worshipper should pray for Jesus' mercy. Lydgate includes also a "lytyll prayer" of his own, that God might give us pardon; that we might be made pleasing to God; that we might come to see God; and that he will continue to show us his mercy.

[11] *Minor Poems I*, pp. 77-84. Lydgate notes: "To symple folk god sent doun his grace/ Them preferrith, & fortherith for meeknesse" (lines 19-20) to encourage which he is doing this paraphrase "nat konnyngly, but affter my symplesse" (line 18).

[12] G. M. Gibson, "Bury St Edmunds, Lydgate and the N-Town Cycle", *Speculum* 56 (1981), 56-90 at p. 59. It has elsewhere been noted how very closely the saints to whom Lydgate addresses his prayers reflect the iconography of chancel screens in his particular part of East Anglia: see E. Duffy, *The Stripping of the Altars* (London and New Haven, 1992), p. 178. These particular references, more than his work for more distant or more rarefied patrons, indicate how very closely Lydgate was tuned in to the fundamental character of East Anglian popular religion as experienced by ordinary lay people.

[13] *Minor Poems I*, p. 260; p. 87.

Very often, however, what Lydgate has to offer, by paraphrase of liturgical texts, is simply what the psalms and canticles, hymns and prayers of the Church already say, in order that the reader might become more fully integrated into the worship of the Church. It is this which particularly justifies the comparison between Lydgate's verse and the elements of spiritual direction. Although it is formal verse, quite abstracted and notoriously latinate in style, this sacred character has nothing whatsoever to do with literary fashion. It simply reflects the daily context from which it comes and which it exists to explain. There is also the moral counsel implied by and sometimes explicit in the verse-lives of the saints, echoing the themes of that twelfth-century manuscript in Lydgate's possession at Bury. There is a passage in his lengthy *Life of St Edmund*, which was written for Henry VI, where Lydgate lists the ancient miracles at the martyr's shrine and then describes with obvious delight a series of miracles from his own day, as if to say to his readers that this vision of the things of faith and holy life really does relate to the world we live in now.[14] More important, however, is the sacramental focus of so much of Lydgate's work, which is a development of its liturgical basis. In particular there is a detailed explanation of the Holy Eucharist, already hinted at in *The Virtues of the Mass*, and of what we would now call the sacrament of reconciliation, or confession.

The Bodleian manuscript which contains Lydgate's annotations has in it this inscription: "Et veniat super nos misericordia tua domine"; in *An Exposition of the Pater Noster* this becomes, "Suffre thy mercy so up-on us spreede, Part to receyue".[15] Speaking elsewhere Lydgate tells of the means by which this mercy is effective: "... be meke confessyoun ... contrite with repentaunce, To the Iesu, I make my passage ... Thy deth thy passioun, thy crosse

[14] Lydgate tells how it has pleased God, "Off oold tyme and now of newe also/ To shewe to yow by notable evidence/ How this martir of royal excellence/ Preferryd is in the hevenly consistorye": C. Horstmann, ed., *Altenglische Legenden* (London, 1881), p. 445, lines 451-54. This passage exists only in later editions of the *Life*, and it reflects a propagandist as well as a theological preoccupation with St Edmund.

[15] *Minor Poems I*, p. 66, lines 199-200.

shall me directe, Which suffredest deth, Iesu, for our trespace".[16] These words are presented as a direct response to the memory of his youthful vision of a bleeding crucifix, a rather lurid but very contemporary image, like all those Netherlandish altarpieces from across the English Channel, which influenced the local East Anglian school of painting. For Lydgate, the sight of Christ's face, on the cross, in torment, leads to a direct compulsion to make confession. In another poem, in a similar context, he goes further, instructing his readers:

And by thy mouth thou make confessyoun
Of thy trespace, man, whyles thou art here
And satisfaccioun thou doo eeke in feere.[17]

That is reasonably directional, however impersonal.

The sufferings of Jesus are at the heart of Lydgate's passion poetry, and these emphases are similar to those in the texts which occur in expensive fifteenth-century devotional manuscripts illustrated with pictures of skeletons and blood to stress the pain and anguish which inspire penitence. For Lydgate these sufferings are

[16] "The Testament": *Minor Poems I*, p. 344, lines 404, 406-7, 418-19.

[17] "A Holy Meditation": *Minor Poems I*, p. 48, lines 172-74. Cf. also "The Pater Noster Translated": *Minor Poems I*, p. 18, stanza 7:

And whateuer offence ys done before
In thought, worde, dede, or countenaunce,
For the furst day that we were bore,
We aske now grace of repentaunce,
And here to performe oure dew penaunce,
Kepyng oure wyttes and thy hestes ten,
And gracious Fadyr take no vengeaunce,
Sed libera nos a malo. Amen;

or this: "The Fifteen Joys of Our Lady": *Minor Poems I*, p. 261, stanza 3:

That I may com to his miserycorde
By confessyon and trewe repentaunce, -
And thow woldest to my request acorde -
Here for my synnes that I may do penannce [sic],
And eke my sowle with helthe so avaunce
That I may with humble and trewe entente,
Or I passe hennys, Resceyue the sacremente.

This final reference reflects also the fundamentally Christocentric and sacramental focus of the Marian verse.

the inspiration for formal confession and penance. This does not mean, however, that his ideas of sinfulness can be reduced to mere formalism: there are places in which his verse contains a teasing out of moral problems that reflects a shrewd psychological awareness which is in keeping with an authentic confessional context:

This to seyne, I can be weell vengable,
Whan my neihbour doth a smal trespace,
Thouh I be gylty and horrybly coupable
Can fynde weies lyghtly for to passe,
Ageyn my brother grete gyltes compasse,
My-silf excuse, and put on him the wrak,
Lyk fawssemblaunt shewe out a fair face
As in my-silf ther founde were no lak.[18]

But equally Lydgate vocalises the thoughts of the dying Christ as he looks down on the penitents before him:

Upon the cros naylled I was ffor the,
Suffred deth to paye thy raunsoun;
Forsake thy senne for the love of me,
Be repentaunt, make pleyn confessioun,
To contrit hertis I do remyssioun:
Be nat dyspeyred, for I am nat vengable;
Geyn goostly enmyes thynk on my passioun;
Why artow froward, sith I am mercyable?[19]

Often these verses end with a plea for the mediation of Mary, and there are times when it is the thought of Our Lady of Sorrows

[18] "Exposition of the Pater Noster": *Minor Poems I*, p. 68, stanza 32.

[19] "A Prayer Upon the Cross": *Minor Poems I*, p. 252, stanza 1. This poem ends, in stanza 5, with a prayer appropriate for genuine confessional use:

Lord on alle synful, heere knelyng on ther kne,
Thy deth remembryng of humble affeccyoun,
O Iesu, graunte of thy benygnyte,
That thy fyve wellis plentyvous of foysoun,
Callid thy fyve woundis by computacioun,
May wasshe in us al surfetis reprevable.
Now, for thy modris meek mediacioun,
At hir request, be to us mercyable.

herself which inspires this spirit of penitence and devotion, but the consistency of the theme and of its expression is, I think, clear.[20]

All these references to the importance of formal confession, however, do not amount to any real evidence that John Lydgate was an ardent sacerdotalist; there is something deep in his temperament which makes this doubtful, and these examples – sometimes, as in *The Testament of Dan John Lydgate*, against himself – indicate that theologically he understood this penitence as a response to the vision of Christ rather than to a rigidly oppressive system of ecclesiastical rules and regulations, however tempting this sort of legalism might have seemed to be in the early fifteenth century, especially as a reaction against popular heresy. Lydgate gives every impression that he relishes lay religion, that he relishes the vernacular, and that he does not take himself too pompously as a priest.

A focus on the body of Christ on the cross points, particularly in the later middle ages, to the Body of Christ on the altar; and something of this Christocentricity which leaves the priest too in a state requiring that same divine mercy, is there in Lydgate's short *Exhortation to Priests when they shall say Mass*:

Ye holy prestes, remembreth in your herte, ...
Quaketh for drede, trembleth with mekenesse,
Lord of lordys when ye shall receyue.
Next remembreth on that other syde
Gayne hys goodnesse, youre gret iniquite,
Peyseth hys mekenesse ageyne your froward pryde,
Voydeth all rancour, thynke on his charyte,
Weyeth his pacience ayenst your cruelte,
Shryuen and contryte aforn with humble entent,
Seye, "Iesu Mercy," knelyng on your kne,
Or ye receue that holy sacrament.[21]

The Body of Christ is the remedy for the sins of us all.

[20] For example, "On the Image of Pity": *Minor Poems I*, p. 297, stanza 1 etc. The text of this poem makes it clear that it was written to stand before a painted image of some sort: cf. note 13 above.

[21] *Minor Poems I*, pp. 84-85, lines 1, 7-16.

Miri Rubin has written about Lydgate's eucharistic poetry and interpreted much of it, such as the prodigious *Procession of Corpus Christi*, as a form of vernacular preaching, inferring from the verse a living pastoral function for the devotional good of his readers.[22] *The Virtues of the Mass* and the *Exposition of the Pater Noster* both offer precise explanations of the ritual and theology of the Mass, and a host of devotional prayers to encourage informed and worthy communion. These works are not to be regarded as poetry *per se*. Verse is merely the medium, written to build up the lay people in a faith which is orthodox and lively. There are, indeed, references in these works to the heretical tendencies of the day, and we might remember the need to keep people like Margery Kempe on the straight and narrow.[23] The *Exposition of the Pater Noster* ought properly to be considered as a fully worked out vernacular catechism, which can stand alongside the English translations of Archbishop Thoresby's more famous *Catechism*, or other contemporary catechistical writings in English, such as the sermon by another Benedictine, John Cateridge of York St Mary's, which is a paraphrase of the same material. These works reflect a very

[22] Miri Rubin, *Corpus Christi* (Cambridge, 1991), pp. 229-32.

[23] For example, "A Defence of Holy Church" in *Minor Poems I*, p. 33, addressed to the king:

> For who is blynde or haltith in the faith
> For any doctryne of these sectys newe,
> And Cristes techyng therfor aside laith,
> Unto thy corone may he nat be trewe.

Cf. "The Legend of St Austin at Compton" in *Minor Poems I*, p. 197, stanza 17, referring to the orthodox faith introduced to this land by St Augustine of Canterbury, and embodied in the Creed:

> Thus he began by grace of Goddis hond,
> Wher God list werche may be noon obstacle,
> By his labour was cristened al this lond,
> Feith of our lord wex moor cleer than spectacle;
> Whan tholygoost made his habitacle
> In tho personys that wern in woord and deede,
> By Awstyn tournyd, that God wrouhte a gret myracle,
> To make hem stable in Articles of the Creede.

This stanza, in particular, offers a very clear hint of the importance of standing firm in the apostolic tradition entrusted to the official Church.

considerable effort on the part of the English bishops to cultivate, with the help of the monks, a pastoral and educational culture within the Church.[24] Of the pastoral importance of these books there can scarcely be much doubt.

Something of the use to which these works were put is indicated in the manuscript copies which survive. There are many manuscripts of Lydgate's verse – much of it secular; some of them contain more or less complete collections of the shorter poems, religious and secular; some are specifically devotional in their purpose. Some are exclusively Marian, and so fall just beyond the scope of the subject of this paper; there are others which contain devotional works by all sorts of authors, with Lydgate chief among them. There are also collections of his psalms and hymns and prayers to saints. Some contain the catechistical material. Others are expensive illustrated volumes which contain texts such as *The Virtues of the Mass* and some of the shorter devotional poems, like a manuscript now in Oxford which lists the names of the distinguished lay women who owned it during the fifteenth century. Another extraordinarily lavish manuscript from the library of the Dominican nuns at Dartford puts some of Lydgate's verse alongside texts by Suso, Adam the Carthusian and Richard Rolle.[25] What these books show is that Lydgate was being used very widely, and by an equally wide range of people, as a guide to the moral and devotional

[24] The text and translations of Archbishop Thoresby's *Catechism* are printed in T. F. Simmons and H. E. Nolloth, eds, *The Lay Folks' Catechism*, EETS os 118 (London, 1901): this volume contains not only the English text of the Archbishop's catechism, but also the Latin of the canons of the Lambeth Council of 1281 on which it was based, the Latin version approved by Thoresby's York convocation in 1357, and a later Lollard paraphrase, again in English. John Cateridge's sermon is printed in G. G. Perry, ed., *Religious Pieces in Prose and Verse*, EETS os 26 (London, 1867; rev. 1914) and like Lydgate's work, demonstrates the very prominent role being played by Benedictines in providing simple devotional and pastoral help for ordinary lay people.

[25] These particular manuscripts are Oxford, Bod. MSS Hatton 73 and Douce 322. The latter manuscript is an especially good example of the mixture of highly speculative spiritual writing with an almost morbid preoccupation with pain and blood and gore which provides the focus for some of its illustrations.

life, and that his work was being consulted for instruction and for help with prayer.

We know that many of Lydgate's patrons were regular visitors to the monastery at Bury as members of the monastic confraternity: the Pastons, the de la Poles, the Beauchamps. We know that the early fifteenth-century Church was concerned to cultivate the articulate religious awareness of its laity and to be an effective agency against the emergent heretical sects. We are now beginning to recognise John Lydgate himself, not only as a poet and verse maker, an encyclopaedist, even a political thinker and early humanist, but also as a Christian man and monk, the author of fully worked-out verse-sermons and books of spiritual counsel. We encounter him in his religious and devotional verse as a devout but humane priest who exhorts his readers to scrutinise their consciences and to make careful confession; who gives them moral guidance; who explains the meaning and significance of the articles of faith and of the customs of the Church; who provides instructions and examples for prayer. All of this amounts to consistent spiritual guidance for his readers. It is for this reason that there should be little cause to doubt that in his personal encounters with lay people, as confessor, teacher and counsellor, John Lydgate was as consistent in his provision of spiritual direction as he was in the verse which so clearly and so fully reflects it.[26]

[26] I am indebted to my friends and colleagues David Shenton and Garry Humphryes for help in preparing this text for publication.

The Influence of Humanism in the Monasticism of Robert Joseph, Monk of Evesham

Anthony Marett-Crosby

This paper examines a broad theme in the history of late medieval monasticism by the use of a single source. Its subject is the relationship between humanism and monasticism, which will be studied using the letters of a single English Benedictine monk, Robert Joseph of Evesham. Robert Joseph was a monk-scholar at Oxford between 1524 and 1530 and again after 1533, between which he returned to live in his monastery at Evesham. There he spent his free hours writing letters, and – more significantly for our purposes – recording those letters in his casual, sometimes illegible script, in a commonplace book.[1]

Out of this collection of letters has come a remarkable and significant academic conclusion. In his magisterial survey of the period, Fr James McConica has argued that the Gloucester College at which Robert Joseph studied was "a place where a monk might learn

[1] The letters are in a single manuscript, National Library of Wales, MS Peniarth 119, fols 504-735. I follow the numbering of both letters and lines of the printed edition: H. Aveling and W. A. Pantin, eds, *The Letter Book of Robert Joseph, Monk-Scholar of Evesham and Gloucester College, Oxford, 1530-3*, Oxford Historical Society, new ser. 19 (Oxford, 1967), henceforth Robert Joseph, *Letters*.

a great deal of Erasmian humanism".[2] This tells us something important about the extent of humanist learning in Oxford, but it also offers a striking insight into the thought-world of monasticism on the eve of the English Reformation, a thought-world apparently impregnated with humanism.

In what did this humanism consist? It is this question that Robert Joseph answers for us in a special way. He is neither a philosopher, nor a theologian, nor a theoretician of monastic life. His letters present us not with a coherent system but with a personality – they allow us to see a monk surrounded by and engaging with his friends. As such, it is with individuals that the student of the letters of Joseph must be concerned, and it is within a prosopographical framework that this paper will proceed. The examination of what humanism meant to Joseph will proceed firstly by comparing him with two humanists, selected by Erasmus as models. Secondly, it will examine those individuals whom Joseph himself selects as being of particular note in regard to their learning, men whom he credits with the epithet *vir humanissimus*.

Robert Joseph's humanist context is best understood by using the two idealised models in the humanist endeavour described by Erasmus in his letter of 1521 addressed to Jodocus Jonas.[3] They are absolutes of the humanist endeavour, against which the humanism of Joseph can fruitfully be compared.

Robert Joseph knew and respected Erasmus enormously. He described Erasmus as being "the glory of our age", and he

[2] James McConica, *English Humanists and Reformation Politics under Henry VIII and Edward VI* (Oxford, 1965), pp. 94; 76-105. Other studies of Robert Joseph include Knowles, *Religious Orders*, 3:100-7; W. A. Bruneau, "Humanism, the University and Monastic Life: The Case of Robert Joseph of Evesham", *British Journal of Education Studies* 20 (1972), 282-301; A. Marett-Crosby, "Robert Joseph and his Letter Book", in *Benedictines in Oxford*, ed. H. Wansbrough and A. Marett-Crosby (London, 1997), pp. 133-54.

[3] Erasmus, *Opus Epistolarum Des. Erasmi Roterodami*, ed. P. S. Allen, H. M. Allen and H. W. Garrod, 12 vols (Oxford, 1906-58), 4:507-27 (Letter to Jodocus Jonas, henceforth Erasmus, *Letter*). There is an English translation in J. C. Olin, *Christian Humanism and the Reformation: Selected Writings* (Gloucester, Mass., 1973), pp. 164-91.

strenuously defended his reputation and cited his writings frequently.[4] It is this evident love of Erasmus in Joseph's letters that is the principal reason for the link between this humble monk of Evesham and the wider world of humanism.[5] We must however be careful to note that Joseph never cites texts from Erasmus indiscriminately, but rather makes very heavy use of a single work. Of eighty-eight quotations from Erasmus contained in the one hundred and seventy-six letters, a staggering seventy-five are from a single work, Erasmus' *Adagia*. By contrast, none of Erasmus' theological works are cited at all, save one reference to his commentary on Psalm 73.

It is quite likely that Robert Joseph had a copy of the *Adagia*, and it was certainly high on his list of recommended reading.[6] But the *Adagia* is a striking and peculiar book. In its final form, which Joseph probably never saw, it came to consist of over 4,000 classical proverbs, each with a historical explanation designed to illustrate how a proverb was used in the authors of antiquity. Alongside these explanations, some of the proverbs are given a contemporary application which is very much Erasmus' own. The purpose of the work was to open a window on to the classical world by making available to the *mediocriter literati* a storehouse of useful – and easily explained – phrases. It offered to its readers a treasury of classical tags, which could be easily used in an appropriate context much as could the contents of the *Vulgaria* composed by the English humanist scholar William Hormann.[7] Hormann arranges his classical references thematically, whereas Erasmus has no order in his collection, but offers a much broader perspective and explanation. Within this text there are certainly some polemical passages, especially on the church, but the *Adagia* is not a polemical work. This reveals how much the relationship between Joseph and Erasmus was not one of theological dependence. It was based on classical learning, and most of Joseph's citations from the *Adagia* consist of either the classical text itself or

[4] Robert Joseph, *Letters*, 24.21ff, 97.2ff. See also Marett-Crosby, "Robert Joseph", pp. 141-44 for humanism and Robert Joseph.

[5] A case overstated by Bruneau, "Humanism", pp. 290-92.

[6] For example, Robert Joseph, *Letters*, 73.11.

[7] William Hormann, *Vulgaria viri doctissimi Guil. Hormann Caesoriburgensis* (London, 1519).

the historical explanation that Erasmus offers. It is an accepted axiom of humanist studies that Erasmus was a man of many parts, and to Joseph he was always a classicist.

It is as models of humanism, and as illustrating humanism lived out within the church, that Jean Vitrier and John Colet are valuable pointers to the kind of humanism that Joseph himself espoused. This is seen in their respective theologies of the Church. Both Vitrier and Colet were loyal sons of the Roman church, and neither they nor Erasmus belonged to the radical edge of sixteenth-century theology.[8] Indeed, Joseph would have found much to admire in their studious avoidance of dissent. When confronted with heretics or with heretical books Joseph's reaction was one of horror mixed perhaps with a certain despair at those who "tear apart the seamless robe of Christ".[9] When confronted with the heresy of William Tracey, Joseph's response was to compare him to the Old Testament figure Samson, doing more harm in his death than he had ever done in his life.[10] Joseph's desire is to avoid controversy at all costs, and one of the most beautiful passages in his letters is his prayer that he may live in peaceful times.[11] It was a prayer destined not to be heard.

In contrast to Joseph's conventional and strictly orthodox view of the Church, Vitrier and Colet are presented by Erasmus as being at odds with traditional forms of religious life, of which the Benedictine way chosen by Joseph was the most traditional of all. Vitrier was an observant Franciscan,[12] but was at variance with his community and spent his old age far away from it. Colet was not a religious, though Erasmus writes that, were he to have found a religious order that lived up to his ideals, he would have joined it. Colet is indeed critical of the orders, not in their institutions but because "those who took

[8] On Erasmus' ecclesiology see the recent contribution by Hilmar Pabel, "The Peaceful People of Christ: the Irenic Ecclesiology of Erasmus of Rotterdam", in *Erasmus' Vision of the Church*, ed. Pabel (Kirksville, Missouri, 1995), pp. 57-93.

[9] Robert Joseph, *Letters*, 165.8.

[10] Robert Joseph, *Letters*, 71.22ff.

[11] Robert Joseph, *Letters*, 165.5ff.

[12] Erasmus, *Letter*, lines 13-16.

vows do not come up to their profession".[13] This mixture of idealism and disappointment with those who fail to live up to this ideal is demonstrated for Erasmus in Colet's reform of the secular chapter of St Paul's Cathedral. He notes that those who opposed these reforms accused him of making it too like a monastery,[14] attempting to impose a discipline which the canons – and perhaps many monks of his day – would have found alien.

Robert Joseph, however, was not and could never have been a reformer. Despite his impatience with the cloister,[15] he evinces no desire to reaffirm the demands of the monastic life, but rather to escape from them by returning to Oxford.[16] He may have referred to his cloister at Evesham as a prison and to his abbot as Pharaoh,[17] but there is not a hint of reforming zeal save perhaps in his impatience with those overlong liturgies that distracted him from letter-writing.[18]

Moreover, Robert Joseph was a vigorous defender of the *status quo*. Thus in his striking correspondence with an Augustinian canon friend, William Dalaam, Joseph shows himself to be an ardent defender of the much criticised monastic diet of the period. Ever since the fourteenth century, when the prohibition on meat eating contained in the Rule of St Benedict had been relaxed,[19] this had been a subject of both contention and satire, and Dalaam, on a visit to Evesham, had apparently expressed his surprise at the extravagance in the refectory fare.[20] Joseph defends this by writing that the kind of asceticism espoused by a church father like Jerome, who had been quoted against him, was simply out of date, and could no longer be

[13] Erasmus, *Letter*, lines 448-49.

[14] Erasmus, *Letter*, lines 534-37.

[15] Robert Joseph, *Letters*, 51.21-22, 53.6-7, 54.19, 86.17-18, 126.1, 147.3.

[16] Robert Joseph, *Letters*, 20.22, 25.5-6, 45.11-12, 46.27-28, 91.4-5, 111.18-19, 115.14-15, 131.1, 147.17.

[17] Robert Joseph, *Letters*, 54.20, 132.25.

[18] See above note 15 and also letters 42.6, 63.26.

[19] Rule of St Benedict, 39.11 (*RB 1980*, p. 238): "Carnium vero quadrupedum omnimodo ab omnibus abstineatur comestio". For the relaxation of this precept, see Knowles, *Religious Orders* 2:1-7, with Peter McDonald, "The Papacy and Monastic Observance in the Later Middle Ages: The Benedictina in England", *Journal of Religious History* 38 (1987), 117-32.

[20] Robert Joseph, *Letters*, 152.13-15.

imposed on monks. He never questions the theoretical value of ascetic fasting, but simply says that it is not for him, and more widely not for the monastic order.[21]

In another way, however, Robert Joseph and the two model humanists agree, for in both there is an exaltation of the priesthood.[22] Vitrier and Colet are presented by Erasmus primarily as priests, though their priesthood is understood in a new way. It is not liturgical or sacramental action which lies at the heart of their priesthood but rather the preaching of the Word, which they do through studious application to the Scriptures and especially to St Paul.[23] Further to this, they are men of moderation, excessive neither in indulgence nor in fasting, and they show themselves ready to dispense with the normal requirements of fasting should that prove necessary for study.[24] Their priesthood is pastoral, determined by the demands of their flock rather than by any absolute devotion to the Mass or to the Divine Office. Colet for one found the latter to be almost an incomprehensible burden.[25]

Robert Joseph speaks of priesthood as the *magna dignitas sacerdotum*,[26] and writing to his fellow monk and friend, John Feckenham, before his ordination he talks of him "taking up the sword of the spirit which is the Word of God".[27] Writing to Robert Dorning he talks of the priest as an example, constantly under the scrutiny of his flock.[28] Elsewhere he praises good preaching, and above all rejoices in the tranquil life that he believes to be the lot of the secular priest. Writing to the Cistercian Humphrey Chester, he says:

[21] Robert Joseph, *Letters*, 152.35-37.

[22] The best recent survey of attitudes to priesthood in the period is Peter Marshall, *The Catholic Priesthood and the English Reformation* (Oxford, 1994).

[23] Erasmus, *Letter*, lines 44-45, 241-43, 282.

[24] Erasmus, *Letter*, lines 98-100, 307-8.

[25] Erasmus, *Letter*, lines 508-11.

[26] Robert Joseph, *Letters*, 75.16.

[27] Robert Joseph, *Letters*, 75.18ff.

[28] Robert Joseph, *Letters*, 77.31-40.

> I cannot see what could be a more peaceful life than that called secular priesthood, [for such a priest] lives in a chaste, holy and humane way.[29]

It was indeed to this life that Robert Joseph came after the dissolution, when Evesham, in company with the other abbeys of England, was torn apart. Joseph was not among those who joined the refounded Westminster community under Queen Mary, though his best friend Feckenham was its first and only abbot.[30] As far as can be seen, Joseph lived out his post-monastic days in precisely this kind of priestly life; the appeal it evidently had for him even in his monastic days perhaps provides a clue as to how it was that so many monks abandoned their monasteries with so little overt complaint.

Another area in which there is some similarity between Robert Joseph and Erasmus' model humanists lies in theology. Both Colet and Vitrier were keen students of Scripture,[31] but only very reluctant scholastics. Both men are recorded as having made use of the writings of Thomas Aquinas and Duns Scotus, but it is always a hesitant use hedged about with cautions as to the inadequacy of what they found.[32] In a brief autobiographical insertion, Erasmus records how he himself had once praised Thomas Aquinas to Colet, only to be told that Thomas was seriously deficient, both because he analysed too much and because he made too much use of the philosophy of the pagans, especially Aristotle.[33] The target of Joseph's criticisms was not Thomas so much as Scotus, and the phrase *Scotist subtleties* is one of the strongest insults in his repertoire.[34] This hostility should not however be exaggerated; Joseph did of course study at Oxford in an overwhelmingly scholastic environment, and at one point he does indeed defend this theological tradition quite vigorously.[35] Like

[29] Robert Joseph, *Letters*, 163.22-24.

[30] On Feckenham's career, see A. B. Emden, *A Biographical Register of the University of Oxford, A.D. 1501-1540* (Oxford, 1974), under Feckenham.

[31] See above note 23.

[32] Erasmus, *Letter*, lines 20-23, 66-68, 274-75.

[33] Erasmus, *Letter*, lines 419-44.

[34] Robert Joseph, *Letters*, 53.33, 112.5-8, 135.17-18, 155.4-5 are examples of such insults.

[35] Robert Joseph, *Letters*, 137.12ff.

Vitrier and Colet, he made use of it, but equally he found it irksome, and perhaps altogether too much like hard work.

If this is humanism, then it is a none too radical version of it. There is a basic loyalty to the church that underpins Robert Joseph as much as it did Vitrier and Colet, a loyalty focused especially upon an exaltation of priesthood.[36] This comparison offers us a context, a context of moderate priestly humanism, into which Robert Joseph seems to fit.

It is now appropriate to examine Robert Joseph's relationship to humanism for a more personal perspective. Among his many correspondents, Joseph identified eight by the use of a special epithet, *vir humanissimus*. To the student searching the corpus for evidence of humanism, this phrase is striking, and may perhaps be taken as a rough guide at least to the kind of people Joseph credited with humane values, values which in a later century might come to be called humanist. The prosopography of this group offers an insight into how Joseph himself conceived the humanist endeavour.

It is appropriate to turn first to those so described who were members of religious orders. There are six of these, beginning with William Dalaam, an Augustinian canon of Studley and subprior of that community in the year 1534. Robert Joseph wrote eight letters to him, mostly relating to that visit to Evesham made by Dalaam in 1532 discussed above. It is to Dalaam that Robert Joseph made his spirited defence of monastic food,[37] but he also chose to send Dalaam a selection of his own verses, no doubt expecting his Augustinian friend to receive them well. He is twice described as *humanissimus*.[38]

A second religious so described is William Jerome,[39] a monk of Winchcombe abbey and an associate of the former abbot of that community, Richard Kidderminster.[40] Robert Joseph writes only one

[36] On Colet and the priesthood, see above note 22.

[37] See above notes 20 and 21.

[38] Robert Joseph, *Letters*, 153.8 and 154.1.

[39] Not the William Jerome of Christ Church, Canterbury, burned in 1540 for his adherence to Lutheranism.

[40] Robert Joseph, *Letters*, 167.1.

letter to Jerome, in which he praises both him and his work, describing the latter as being *humanissimus*.[41]

A third individual is also a Benedictine. Robert Joseph wrote twice to the monk John Harriss, monk of Tavistock. He was known to many of Joseph's friends, and Joseph seems to have come to know him through John Feckenham.[42] It was to Feckenham, however, rather than to Harriss himself that Robert Joseph described him as *humanissiumus*.[43]

A fourth religious in this category is Feckenham himself.[44] It is impossible in this context to do justice to this most renowned member of Robert Joseph's circle, the future dean of St Paul's and abbot of the restored Westminster abbey. At this time, Feckenham was simply a monk of Robert Joseph's own community of Evesham, a student at Gloucester College, Oxford, during the time of the correspondence. Robert Joseph's letters to this, his closest friend, are perhaps the last outpouring of that tradition of monastic friendship going back to Anselm and Peter of Celles. Among the various praises is that of *humanissimus*, applied to Feckenham's letters.[45]

The final two religious in this category are more difficult to identify. Almost certainly a religious, but of an unidentified order and house is Simon Sotharne, to whom Robert Joseph wrote only once in this period but who was probably the eventual executor of his will in 1569.[46] He was the recipient of Joseph's most curious piece of work, a series of twelve bookplate inscriptions in verse form. In an accompanying letter, he praises Sotharne as an author known by his *humanissimis literis*.[47] The final religious is known only by his place of origin. In letter 12, to the Cistercian monk, Philip Acton,[48] Robert Joseph sends his greetings to one Evesham,[49] presumably the same

[41] Robert Joseph, *Letters*, 169.3.

[42] Robert Joseph, *Letters*, 91.27, 99.11, 131.20 for Harriss among his friends.

[43] Robert Joseph, *Letters*, 92.37.

[44] See above note 30.

[45] Robert Joseph, *Letters*, 131.13.

[46] On the will, see Appendix 4 of Robert Joseph, *Letters*, pp. 267-68.

[47] Robert Joseph, *Letters*, 64.4.

[48] The recipient of 4 of his letters.

[49] Robert Joseph, *Letters*, 12.28.

Evesham to whom he later writes in letter 26. Acton was a monk of Hailes, and this link led Aveling and Pantin in their biographical notes to tentatively identify this correspondent as a monk of Hailes.[50] Letter 26 does not confirm this, and rather suggests a link between him and a monk of Abingdon, Gabriel Clement.[51] There was a Richard Evesham, a monk of Evesham abbey, who became prior of Abingdon between 1534 and 1538, and a remark in letter 26 does indeed suggest that the recipient may have been a monk of Robert Joseph's own community. Exact identification must remain uncertain,[52] but he is described in the first line of the letter as being a *vir humanissimus*.[53]

Two other recipients of this title are not religious but secular masters. The first is Edward Grexon, a fellow of two Cambridge colleges but by 1532 the rector of Fladbury in Worcestershire.[54] He is the recipient of all of Robert Joseph's superlatives, including that of *vir humanissimus*.[55] So also is Henry Wyllys,[56] a fellow of Corpus Christi College, Oxford, and perhaps also vicar of Toddington. He may have been related to Joseph, and was the recipient of seven letters from him. He was the author of some witty sermon notes that Robert Joseph sought, and is praised for his erudition as *vir humanissimus*.[57]

What is immediately clear is that six of the eight men labelled in this special way are religious. Robert Joseph's correspondents were mostly monks, and of those monks many were from his own community.[58] We should be wary of assuming that the world in which he lived stretched far beyond cloister and order. It is striking that of all the letters he wrote to Oxford, for example, none were received by

[50] Robert Joseph, *Letters*, p. 274.

[51] Robert Joseph, *Letters*, 26.21-22.

[52] See above note 50.

[53] Robert Joseph, *Letters*, 26.1.

[54] Robert Joseph, *Letters*, p. 276.

[55] Robert Joseph, *Letters*, 150.15, 151.22.

[56] Robert Joseph, *Letters*, p. 285.

[57] Robert Joseph, *Letters*, 27.1.

[58] Of the 166 letters whose addressee is certain, 98 are either to Benedictine or Cistercian monks. Of those letters addressed to Oxford correspondents, 54 out of 77 are to monks.

any religious who were not also Benedictines. There is not a mention in any of his letters of the friars and other religious who were attracted to that city – it is as if they did not exist.

The second striking fact is that these eight cannot be described as being a university elite. Four of the eight are known to have held degrees, and one other was also resident for a time at Gloucester College, but three have left no mark on the university records at all.[59] More important is the fact that none of the eight are actually friends made by Robert Joseph at Oxford. They do not belong to Joseph's university world at all, but rather to the world of his cloister. Two of them are of his own community, one is possibly of his own family, and a further one is known to Joseph only through Feckenham.[60] Of the others, it is striking that they are local contacts from the Evesham area. There is no reason to think that Joseph knew the Cambridge master Edward Grexon before he was rector of Fladbury, and others too among the eight lived close by. Fladbury is four miles from Evesham, while Toddington where Wyllys may have lived was only eight miles away. Dalaam's Studley priory was twenty miles from Evesham, but he had no connection with Oxford or Cambridge at all of which we know. The only letters sent to Oxford amongst those received by the eight were addressed to Feckenham, his monastic colleague from Evesham.

This begs the question of what indeed the epithet *humanissimus* implied for Robert Joseph. In the case of both religious and seculars it refers in the first place to the quality of their letter-writing. Dalaam, Evesham, Feckenham, Grexon and Wyllys are all praised for this quality, and in consequence are told of Joseph's own weakness in this regard.[61] The bookplates he sent to Sotharne were exercises in good writing, as were the verses sent to Dalaam.[62] In another letter to Dalaam, Joseph indeed identifies the cultivation of decent Latin as

[59] The three are William Dalaam, William Jerome and Simon Sotharne.

[60] The suggestion that Henry Wyllys was a relative of Robert Joseph is made in Robert Joseph, *Letters*, pp. xxiv, 285.

[61] Robert Joseph, *Letters*, 140.3, 26.7, 75.9-10, 92.5-7, 151.2, 71.20-21.

[62] Robert Joseph, *Letters*, letters 65 and 148.

one of the main purposes of letter-writing, and it was probably in order to preserve a record of good style that he kept the letter book.[63]

This then was the humanist endeavour. Texts like the *Adagia* of Erasmus or the *Vulgaria* of William Hormann were part of the humanist scholarly output, and the Latin which Robert Joseph loved was indeed the Latin of the classics, not that of the scholastics. He condemned the style of the latter as being simply barbarism.[64] But Joseph's correspondents, at least those whom he styles *viri humanissimi*, demonstrate no wider humanist agenda. Their talk is peppered with conventional piety, with the Mass, the dispute over food at Evesham, the promise of prayers. They show Joseph and his friends as quite unconcerned with the reform of the Benedictine life.

In the case of the seculars whom Robert Joseph styles in this way, there is another element. The only occasions when Joseph comes into contact with the shadowy world of sixteenth-century heresy are in connection with these two seculars, Grexon and Wyllys. Grexon sent Joseph a heretical book, while it was to Wyllys that Joseph described the errors of William Tracey.[65] There was a world of new views beyond the cloister, and some of those whom Joseph praises are in contact with it. But he himself is quite removed from it. There is no attachment to either a new theology or to a new ecclesiology, and he remains secure within the theological mindset of medieval man, in which dissent places one outside the fold of the church. Some humanists, and perhaps especially Erasmus, agreed, but his lack even of interest in these new ideas surely places Joseph apart from his master. For him, and for those around him, the humanist endeavour consisted of good Latin, in a selective classicism and little else.

Robert Joseph's world was one shaped by his experience at Oxford, but not critically determined by it. His friends, and especially those whom he labelled as humane men, were not in fact Oxford contacts at all, but in various ways connected to Evesham either by ties of patronage or religious profession. The world of the new

[63] Robert Joseph, *Letters*, 149.14-17. This is discussed further in Marett-Crosby, "Robert Joseph", pp. 134-41.

[64] Robert Joseph, *Letters*, 21.10.

[65] Robert Joseph, *Letters*, 71.22.

learning was immensely appealing, because it offered them a purer form of Latin and a classical world in which they could immerse themselves. The frustration they felt with their religious life was probably quite unconnected with this, and the wider world of new thinking, of new theology and of dissent, was to them utterly alien. Their humanism did not lead away from monasticism, nor even towards its reform.

Unsafe Passage: The State of the Nuns at the Dissolution and their Conversion to Secular Life

Marilyn Oliva

The conversion from monastic to secular life for the religious personnel displaced by the suppression of the monasteries has a long and lively historiography. Numbers of nuns, monks, canons, and friars have been bandied about; and their moral state has been alternatively seen as corrupt, exhausted, or fictionalised by the royal commissioners whose job it was to evaluate the integrity of their religious lives. The options available to those turned out have been discussed, as have the monetary compensations awarded to them by the Crown. In addition, numerous ex-religious have been traced through episcopal registers and pension lists from the 1550s and 1560s which have provided a great deal of information about what eventually happened to the people whose lives were in many cases irrevocably changed.[1]

Most historians agree that the changes imposed on the female monastic population were significantly more drastic than they were

[1] For example, G. Baskerville, *English Monks and the Suppression of the Monasteries* (New Haven, 1937); A. G. Dickens, *The English Reformation* (New York, 1964); Hodgett, "Unpensioned Ex-religious", pp. 195-202; Knowles, *Religious Orders in England*, vol. 3; G. W. O. Woodward, *The Dissolution of the Monasteries* (New York, 1966); Youings, *Dissolution*.

for their male counterparts.[2] But even while acknowledging this fact, most scholars have dismissed the nuns and their fates as insignificant either because they were old and decrepit and so did not have long to suffer whatever negative changes in their lifestyles the dissolution may have caused, or because they came from high status social groups which could afford to welcome their religious kin back into the folds of family and friends.[3] The particulars of the nuns' lives have been overlooked and we are thus left with an area of monastic history which invites further investigation.

What I would like to address is how the female religious, primarily the 133 nuns who lived in the diocese of Norwich, made the transition to life outside their convents: what kinds of tools and opportunities helped them change from vowed cloistered women to ones engaged in the temporal world beyond their priories' walls.[4] A number of factors affected the nuns' conversion to secular life: their ages at the time their monasteries were closed, financial arrangements made on their behalf by the Crown, and their social status. While I concentrate particularly on the nuns from the eleven female houses in the Norwich diocese it is possible to compare the Norwich nuns' experiences of this transformation to those of nuns from Yorkshire, London, and Middlesex.[5] Such a comparison not only sheds tremendous light on a relatively opaque subject, it also

[2] Hodgett, "Unpensioned Ex-religious", p. 201; Retha Warnicke, *Women of the English Renaissance and Reformation* (London, 1983), pp. 69-70.

[3] Geoffrey Baskerville, "The Dispossessed Religious after the Suppression of the Monasteries", in *Essays Presented to Reginald Lane Poole* ed. Henry W. Davis (Oxford, 1927), pp. 436-65 at p. 461; Claire Cross, "The Religious Life of Women in Sixteenth-Century Yorkshire", in *Women in the Church*, ed. W. S. Sheils and Diana Wood, Studies in Church History 27 (London, 1990), pp. 307-24; Dickens, *English Reformation*, pp. 245-46.

[4] For how this figure was determined see my book, *The Convent and the Community in Late Medieval England* (Woodbridge, 1998).

[5] Claire Cross and Noreen Vickers, *Monks, Friars and Nuns in Sixteenth Century Yorkshire*, Yorkshire Archaeological Society Record Series, 150 (1995); Catherine Paxton, "The Nunneries of London and Its Environs in the Later Middle Ages" (unpublished D.Phil. dissertation, University of Oxford, 1992); John Tillotson, *Marrick Priory: A Nunnery in Late Medieval Yorkshire*, Borthwick Papers no. 75 (York, 1989).

suggests a pattern of specifically female piety, aspects of which indicate that gender influenced the conversion to secular life of both female and male religious.

All but two of the diocese's female houses were suppressed in 1536 when houses worth less than £200 were closed. Only Bruisyard abbey – one of the four houses of Poor Clares in the country – and Shouldham priory, the diocese's only Gilbertine monastery, stayed open, both until 1539. The majority of the nuns, then, were displaced in this first wave of suppressions. By contrast, though nearly half of the female houses country-wide survived this first set of closings, fewer nuns were affected by the suppressions of 1536 than those which occurred in subsequent years.[6]

Most of the diocese's nuns were relatively young when thus turned out. The seven nuns at Campsey Ash gave their ages at the priory's last episcopal visitation in 1532: most were in their mid-thirties four years later when their house was dissolved.[7] Many more nuns must also have been around 35 years old when their convents were suppressed: five of the eleven prioresses, for example, lived until the mid-1560s, and several nuns of Shouldham priory lived through the 1550s and 1560s.[8] Using the nuns' own testimonies about their ages, and the evidence gleaned from wills and mid-sixteenth-century pension lists allows us to estimate that in the

[6] By my count, approximately 65 female houses were suppressed in 1536 and around 70 closed between 1539 and 1540. See also Kathleen Cooke, "The English Nuns and the Dissolution", in *The Cloister and the World: Essays in Medieval History in Honour of Barbara Harvey*, ed. John Blair and Brian Golding (Oxford, 1996), pp. 287-301 at p. 294.

[7] Augustus Jessopp, ed., *Visitations of the Diocese of Norwich, 1492-1532*, Camden Society, new ser. 43 (London, 1888), pp. 291-92.

[8] Geoffrey Baskerville, "Married Clergy and Pensioned Religious in Norwich Diocese, 1555", *English Historical Review* 48 (1933), 43-64, 199-228 at 208, 210, and 214 for the prioresses of Bungay, Shouldham, and Thetford and the nuns of Shouldham respectively. See Norfolk Record Office (henceforth NRO), Archdeaconry of Norwich burial register of the parish of St Clements, fol. 4, for the prioress of Carrow; and NRO, Norwich Consistory Court 235 Bircham for the prioress of Redlingfield.

diocese of Norwich, the average age of a nun was 32 when most of these female monasteries fell in 1536.[9]

Many nuns elsewhere also survived the dissolution of their houses by decades. The ages of 165 superiors and nuns from seventeen female convents shows that while a few women were over sixty years old, the median age of a nun in England at this time was 40, older than the average age of the female monastic population in the diocese of Norwich (Table 1). The ages of twelve nuns from Thicket priory in Yorkshire represent the range of ages at convents elsewhere: 3 nuns were in their twenties; 3 in their thirties; 3 in their forties; and 2 in their early sixties.[10] Of all the nuns whose ages can be determined accurately, 3 percent were between 15 and 20 years old; approximately 28 percent were between 20 and 30; 27 percent between 30 and 40 years of age; 15 percent were between 40 and 50; 10 percent were between 51 and 60; 15 percent were over 61 years of age.[11]

These first displaced nuns had two options: they could either be released from their vows or request transfers to other convents which remained open until later dates, like Bruisyard and Shouldham. But unlike the majority of nuns elsewhere in England who were expelled from their convents in 1536, only a handful of nuns in the diocese of Norwich chose to be moved to another convent and remain cloistered: three from Marham abbey, the only Cistercian convent for women in the diocese; four from Carrow priory, the only urban female monastic foundation in the diocese; and one nun from the very small and poor fenland priory at

[9] Oliva, *Convent and Community*, pp. 46, 190.

[10] J. S. Purvis, ed., *A Selection of Monastic Rentals and Dissolution Papers*, in *Miscellanea III*, Yorkshire Archaeological Society Record Series, 80 (1931), p. 161.

[11] Numerous other nuns' exact ages are not known but that they lived well beyond the suppression of their houses suggests that they too were relatively young when their houses were dissolved. Jane Wadham, late sexton of Romsey abbey, for example, was young enough when her house was closed to have borne children by 1543: Diana Coldicott, *Hampshire Nunneries* (Ipswich, 1989), p. 146.

Crabhouse.[12] Most of these nuns opted for life outside the convent, but the relative youth of all of the diocese's nuns – even those who chose to stay in religious life for another few years – meant that they all faced potentially long and uncertain futures. Among their most pressing concerns when converting from monastic to secular life then must have been how to support themselves.

Financial support by the government for the majority of nuns was very limited: in the first round of closures arrangements for life-time annual pensions were made for superiors only. Pensions for rank-and-file nuns were not officially legislated until 1537, and so most of the nuns received only a single reward from the Crown, small sums of money which varied in amount both among the nuns of a particular house and also among the various monasteries in general. At Blackborough priory, for example, four nuns received 26s 8d; four others 20s.[13] Two of the Marham nuns also received 26s 8d, while two others from this small abbey took away 45s each.[14] These variations may have reflected a convent's internal hierarchy, whereby senior nuns received higher awards than younger ones, but every one of the nuns from Redlingfield were paid 23s 4d, and some were more senior than others.[15] Whatever the reason, these rewards average out to a little over £2 a piece, amounts which no doubt initially helped ease this transition, but which could not have sustained these ex-religious for very long.

Those in the diocese of Norwich who received life-time pensions were nine superiors, the nuns of Shouldham priory, and at least two nuns from Bungay priory. Pension amounts were not fixed by any legislative body but rather left to the discretion of the royal commissioners who, historians have suggested, used the *Valor*

[12] Woodward, *Dissolution of the Monasteries*, p. 74 estimated that 85% of the nuns displaced in 1536 requested transfers to other religious houses. Augustus Jessopp, "The Norfolk Monasteries at the Time of the Suppression by Henry VIII", in *The Norfolk Antiquarian Miscellany*, ed. Walter Rye (Norwich, 1883), p. 245 (Carrow); PRO, Suppression Papers 5/3/35 (Crabhouse); PRO, E 117/14/22 (Marham).

[13] PRO, Suppression Papers 5/4/130-50.

[14] PRO, E 315/405.

[15] PRO, Suppression Papers 5/3/116.

Ecclesiasticus, that great sixteenth-century audit of all of the country's monasteries, as a guide. And to a certain extent, the superiors' pensions corresponded to the wealth of their particular priories (Table 2). Ela Buttery, the prioress of Campsey Ash, the wealthiest of all the female houses in the diocese, for example, obtained an annual pension of £23 6s 8d, more than any of the other superiors in the diocese received.[16] This correlation between her pension and the priory's value may not only have reflected the convent's greater wealth, but could also have resulted from the royal and aristocratic patronage this house enjoyed throughout its history, which perhaps enhanced Buttery's reputation among her colleagues.[17] At the lowest end of the scale, the prioress of Crabhouse, the smallest and poorest of these female houses, received the least amount of money, only £4.

Most of the other superiors obtained small sums which were relative to the wealth of their houses. But two examples suggest that a convent's estimated wealth did not alone determine how much prioresses – or, in fact, rank-and-file nuns – received. After Ela Buttery, the next largest pension was awarded to Grace Sampson, the last prioress of Redlingfield priory in Suffolk, who received £13 6s 8d. While not the poorest female house in the diocese, it was far from wealthy – being valued at only £67 – and heavily in debt when closed down. Equally curious is the comparatively small amount awarded to Elizabeth Fincham, the last prioress of Shouldham: her house ranked second after Campsey Ash in wealth, but she received a pension of only £5.

Circumstances particular to these two priories suggest some reasons for the disparities between these superiors' pensions and the wealth of their convents. Edmund and Grace Bedingfield, two of Redlingfield's most generous patrons who also acquired this small Benedictine house after its suppression, allowed Sampson to stay in her old quarters.[18] Perhaps they also intervened on her behalf to the royal commissioners for a pension larger than the amount they may

[16] PRO, E 314/54. All subsequent superiors' pension amounts are from this document.

[17] Oliva, *Convent and Community*, chapter 6, especially pp. 169, 172.

[18] NRO, Norwich Consistory Court 235 Bircham for her will.

have been considering. Shouldham was a double house of nuns and canons, and despite the fact that it was founded primarily for nuns with canons attached as adjuncts to serve them, the prior there received a pension of £20 a year while, as we have seen, Elizabeth Fincham received only £5. Could the commissioners' assignment of pensions to the superiors of Shouldham have reflected the inferior status accorded to women by both medieval society and the Church?

Pensions given to superiors of female houses in other parts of England corresponded more closely to their estimated value, and ranged from the £100 annual pension awarded to the abbess of Wilton, whose house was worth more than £600, to the amount received by the prioress of Arden.[19] She was given a pension of £4, but her house was appraised at only £12.[20]

In dioceses throughout England, the pensions awarded by the Crown to female monastic superiors were considerably more substantial than the amounts most of the rank-and-file nuns received. Their pensions, like the awards doled out to the nuns dislodged in 1536, also varied among the nuns of a particular house. Four of the Shouldham nuns obtained annually 40s, while another received only 13s 4d.[21] Two ex-Bungay nuns were pensioned by the Crown, despite the claim by Thomas, Duke of Norfolk, that by the time he arrived to requisition the priory and its possessions, all of the nuns had disappeared, thereby forfeiting their rights to any money from him, the Crown or its agents.[22] Mary Loveday and Elizabeth Duke received 60s and 40s respectively; another Bungay nun, Katherine Hubbert, appears in a 1569 pension list as having had a pension of 40s a year.[23]

[19] Dugdale, *Monasticon*, 2:330-31.

[20] Cross and Vickers, *Monks, Friars and Nuns*, p. 524 for Arden. See also Cooke, "English Nuns", p. 289 for Table 13.1 which shows the relations between superiors' pensions and their convents' wealth for those houses worth more than £200.

[21] PRO, E 101/533/4.

[22] *Letters and Papers, Henry VIII*, 10:241 no. 599, 514, no. 1236; and Sybil Jack, "The Last Days of the Smaller Monasteries in England", *Journal of Ecclesiastical History* 21 (1970), 97-124 at p. 102.

[23] PRO, E 101/533/4 (Loveday and Duke); PRO, E 178/3251 (Hubbert).

A few of the diocese's other ex-nuns procured life-time pensions, but not from the Crown. In his will of 1557, Nicholas Hare directed his wife Katherine to maintain the support of Margaret Loveday, Florence Rouse, Florence Scuteler, and Jane Wentworth, all ex-nuns of Bruisyard abbey, which the Hares had purchased from the Crown in 1539.[24] Payments of 53s were to be continued to three of these women, and one was to be paid 20s. Hare appears to have been the only new owner of these recently dissolved female monasteries to support the ex-nuns. Though not very common, other examples of new owners paying the ex-religious' pensions are known for female houses in other parts of the country. At Thicket priory in Yorkshire, for example, William Wytheham paid pensions of between 33s and 20s to each of the eleven ex-nuns there.[25]

Pension amounts awarded to 824 rank and file nuns from other convents in England also varied among nuns of individual houses. Three of the Marrick priory nuns, for example, received 20s per year; three others 26s 8d; four nuns secured 40s; one received 53s 4d, and another 66s 8d.[26] Such variations notwithstanding, these nuns' pensions also exhibited a more positive relation to their convents' values. Marrick was valued at only £48, but at Elstow abbey, a much wealthier female monastery, each nun procured 53s 4d a year for the rest of their lives.[27]

The pensions awarded to all of the country's ex-female religious averaged 33s 4d, less than the 47s average for the nuns in

[24] PRO, Prerogative Court of Canterbury Probate 11/39/46.

[25] J. Clay, ed., *Yorkshire Monasteries: Suppression Papers*, Yorkshire Archaeological Society Record Series, 48 (1912), p. 161. For another example of nuns' pensions provided by a source other than the Crown, see J. Raine, ed., *Wills and Inventories from the Registry of the Archdeaconry of Richmond, 1442-1579*, Surtees Society, 26 (1853), p. 143 for the case of Anne Lademan, an ex-nun from one of the convents in the county of Richmond, who was owed money from the executors of a Dr. Dakins who seems to have been responsible for her pension.

[26] *Letters and Papers, Henry VIII*, 15:547; Clay, *Yorkshire Monasteries*, pp. 134-35.

[27] *Valor Ecclesiasticus*, 5:67 (Marrick); *Letters and Papers, Henry VIII*, 14(2):24-25 for Elstow which was valued at more than £284.

the diocese of Norwich. The lesser national average might have reflected the large number of very poor houses in the diocese of York, for example, which brought down the overall average of pension amounts for all nuns. If this is true, then the values of female houses in other parts of England showed a stronger connection to the pensions given to the nuns than did those in the diocese of Norwich.

Like their female counterparts, many of the monks and canons in the diocese of Norwich whose houses were closed in 1536 were not pensioned by the Crown. Many were, however, provided for by the Dukes of Norfolk and Earls of Suffolk, who acquired most of the male houses dissolved at this time, and who – despite the Duke of Norfolk's disinclination to accommodate the nuns of Bungay – invested these men with other ecclesiastical positions rather than give them life-time annual pensions.[28] Even a cursory look at the records – primarily the episcopal registers – shows that the male religious in the diocese of Norwich – and in other dioceses as well – procured other benefices as their houses were being suppressed. Because the cathedral priory of Norwich was changed to a dean and chapter, for example, some of the monks there and in several of the priory's cells remained safely in priestly life as deans and prebendaries.[29] But even men whose houses were not adopted into institutions of the reformed church in England secured other benefices which eased their passage from monastic to secular life.[30] William Mexall, an Austin canon of the priory of the Holy Sepulchre in Thetford, became rector of Barningham Norwood; at least two canons of the Premonstratensian abbey of Wendling obtained parochial offices not far from the abbey in the same year of its suppression.[31]

Opportunities for other ecclesiastical positions made the transition for the male religious much less precarious than it was for

[28] Baskerville, "Married Clergy", pp. 202-3.

[29] Dugdale, *Monasticon*, 4:8 (Norwich cathedral priory); for other examples: *ibid.*, pp. 461-62 for Aldeby priory; *ibid.*, pp. 618-19 for Hoxne priory; and *ibid.*, p. 462 for the priory at Lynn.

[30] Baskerville, "Married Clergy", pp. 201-2.

[31] Baskerville, "Married Clergy", p. 200 note 2.

the nuns in the diocese who were turned out in 1536 for whom such options were not available. In fact, benefices were not only available to the monks and canons affected by the early closures, but also to those impacted by later dissolutions when pensions were allowed for all of the ex-religious. Many of the diocese's monks and canons then not only took up new offices, they also received life-time pensions from the Crown which of course ensured the male religious a very safe passage from their monastic to post-dissolution lives.[32]

In contrast to the nuns in the diocese, moreover, the male religious were usually pensioned at a higher rate. We have already seen the disparity between the pensions of the prioress and prior of Shouldham priory: recall that Elizabeth Fincham received £5 per year while Robert Swift received £20 in addition to being given the vicarage of Watlington.[33] The amounts awarded to both the nuns and the canons of this Gilbertine house show a similar inequity: the nuns received between 13s and 40s a year for the rest of their lives; each of the eight canons of the priory procured annual pensions of 54s 4d.[34] A comparison of the pensions of male monastic superiors, monks and canons of other houses in the diocese with those of the prioresses and nuns shows the same pattern. The prior of West Acre took in £40, and the monks at Walsingham received pensions of at least £5 each.[35] While many of these greater amounts obviously reflected the male monasteries' relatively greater wealth – West Acre was valued at £260, and Walsingham at £391 – even monks from poor houses took in more money than did nuns from convents

[32] For the alternatives available and taken up by the ex-male religious in the diocese of Norwich and elsewhere, see Baskerville, *English Monks*, pp. 182-86, 251-52; Gasquet, *Henry VIII and the English Monasteries*, pp. 447-51; Hodgett, "Unpensioned Ex-religious", pp. 195-202; Knowles, *Religious Orders*, 3:389-92; S. Sheppard, "The Reformation and the Citizens of Norwich", *Norfolk Archaeology* 38 (1983), 44-58 at p. 47; and Woodward, *Dissolution of the Monasteries*, pp. 147-49.

[33] PRO, E 101/533/4 for pension amounts; Baskerville, "Married Clergy", p. 200 note 4 for the vicarage.

[34] PRO, E 101/533/4 for the prior's and canons' pensions.

[35] *VCH Norfolk*, 2:404; Baskerville, "Married Clergy", p. 211.

of comparable worth.[36] The average pension a monk or canon received in the diocese was £6, slightly higher than the national average for the male religious of £5 – more than three times what any of their female counterparts procured.[37]

The male religious' larger monetary awards surely signalled men's greater status in both medieval society and the Church; but the point here is that these greater amounts also must have made the transition to secular life for the monks and canons much easier than it was for most of the diocese's ex-nuns. And that many of the ex-male religious had the option to pick up other ecclesiastical positions – the income from which did not jeopardise their post-dissolution pensions – indicates that their fates were at the outset more secure.[38]

Faced with little or no financial support the nuns had very few options. While released from their vows of obedience and poverty, the women were still bound to their vow of chastity until 1549. Examples of ex-nuns who opted to marry despite their enduring oath to be chaste are rare, and though some of the diocese's nuns may have married, there is no evidence to indicate when or to whom. Though name changes would of course make it difficult to track these women, it appears that the unmarried status of the Norwich nuns was representative of nuns elsewhere. Claire Cross and Noreen Vickers, for example, found only six out of 216 nuns in Yorkshire who had married after their monasteries were closed.[39]

Some of the Norwich nuns could have turned to family members for help in making the change from the life of a nun to one of a secular woman, as some of their counterparts elsewhere did. Elizabeth Craike, an ex-nun of Wilberfoss in Yorkshire, for

[36] Baskerville, "Married Clergy", p. 212 for the Weybourne canons who received £3 annually from the Crown and their priory was worth only £28. For the values of these male monasteries, see *Valor Ecclesiasticus, passim.*

[37] Knowles, *Religious Orders*, 3:406-7.

[38] Margaret Bowker, "Henrician Reform and the Parish Clergy", in *The English Reformation Revised*, ed. Christopher Haigh (Cambridge, 1987), pp. 75-93.

[39] Cross and Vickers, *Monks, Friars, and Nuns*, pp. 540, 546, 561, 582, 593, and 607.

example, was remembered in her mother's will of 1548 with an annuity of £3 6s 8d in addition to enough bedding, linen, and household supplies – pots and pans, beds, carpets, and chests – to furnish living quarters.[40] A few examples of family support can also be found among the former nuns from the London houses as well.[41] Most of these women had families who could either afford to provide annual income for their ex-religious kin or had the resources to take them in.[42]

Few examples of this kind of familial support exist, however, among the ex-nuns of any of the houses in the diocese of Norwich. Philip Calthorpe bequeathed to his daughter Dorothy, a nun at Bruisyard, an annual rent of 40s for her life, in 1532.[43] And Jane Drury, also from Bruisyard, came from a family of sufficient means to title herself "gentlewoman" in her will.[44] Most of the diocese's nuns, though, were from families lower on the social scale for whom such support was not possible, or at least not easily proffered.[45] More commonly for these women perhaps were the sentiments expressed by Roger Gigges who left his sister Margaret, a nun of Blackborough, 20s in 1534 "if she lives".[46] His uncertainty about whether or not his sister was dead or alive indicates just how removed from their relatives nuns could be.

Without much financial support from the Crown and perhaps separated too long from their families, most of these nuns had to

[40] Cross and Vickers, *Monks, Friars, and Nuns*, p. 545.

[41] Paxton, "Nunneries of London", pp. 105-6. F. C. and P. Morgan, "Some Nuns, Ex-religious and Former Chantry Priests Living in the Diocese of Hereford (c. 1554)", *Woolhope Naturalists Field Club Transactions*, 27 (1963), pp. 139 and 145 note 3, for Joan Scudamore, the last prioress of Aconbury, who went to live with her family after her priory was closed; no reference is given for this.

[42] See also Raine, *Wills and Inventories*, p. 191 for Cristianna Burgh, alias Dame Peres, last prioress of Nunkeeling who received a pension of £8 and retired to the North Riding of Yorkshire to be with her family.

[43] NRO, Norwich Consistory Court 197 Platfoote.

[44] NRO, Norwich Consistory Court 93-4 Cooke.

[45] For the relatively lesser social rank of the majority of nuns from the diocese of Norwich, see my *Convent and Community*, chapter 2.

[46] NRO, Norwich Consistory Court 256-58 Attmere.

find some means of support. Two ex-nuns from Campsey Ash ran a school together not far from their convent in the town of Dunwich.[47] Several other ex-nuns also moved to towns where employment opportunities were better than in the countryside where most of the diocese's female houses were located. Joan Dereham, a former nun of Shouldham, moved nearby to the town of Lynn; and many others, including Elizabeth Hoth and Ela Buttery, the last prioresses of Thetford and Campsey Ash, moved to the city of Norwich.[48]

Wherever they moved, most of these nuns had to set up their own households, like Jane Wentworth, an ex-Shouldham nun, for example, who purchased a "little tenement" in Framingham.[49] To outfit their new dwellings, some of the former nuns from Flixton priory purchased many of the convent's household furnishings: beds, pillows, coverlets; one nun bought "all the stuff in the fraytor".[50] Grace Sampson, the last prioress of Redlingfield, bought all of the goods in the priory's "new chamber" for 10s.[51] Help in furnishing their new rooms came also from concerned outsiders like John Waterman who bequeathed his best feather bed, a pair of his best sheets, a blanket, and three pillows to Joan Bond, once a nun at Carrow.[52] Bequests like this one continued to be made to former nuns well into the middle of the sixteenth century.[53]

While single living was clearly an option, though not an easily affordable one, many of the diocese's ex-nuns continued to live together in their new locations which undoubtedly helped to smooth their way into secular life. Several mid-century wills include bequests to ex-nuns of Carrow priory who were sharing quarters in

[47] NRO, Norwich Consistory Court 520-521 Popy for Thomas Robert's will where he mentions that they rent a room from him "where they keep school".

[48] PRO, E 178/3251 (Dereham); Baskerville, "Married Clergy", pp. 210 (Hoth), 205 (Buttery).

[49] Baskerville, "Married Clergy", p. 219.

[50] PRO, Suppression Papers 5/1/110.

[51] PRO, Suppression Papers 5/3/133.

[52] NRO, Norwich Consistory Court 75-77 Wymer.

[53] See for example, NRO, Norwich Consistory Court 275-78 Mingay (1542); NRO, Norwich Consistory Court Punting (1545); NRO, Norwich Consistory Court 51-52 Hyll (1537).

the Norwich city parish of St Peter Hungate. Joan Bond, for example, was living with Cecily Suffield who had been prioress of Carrow at its dissolution.[54] At least two of the Shouldham nuns continued to live together in another of the city's parishes, St Stephen's, where Ela Buttery also resided until her death in 1546.[55] Interestingly, these two parishes had been sites of informal communities of religious women in the fifteenth century.[56]

Financial necessity certainly must have influenced the women's choice to remain together after their houses were closed, but a sense of community and identity with other ex-female religious must also have been a factor in this decision. Perhaps staying together was the only way they could continue to maintain any kind of religious life. The new church in England did not allow religious orders for women, which thereby restricted them to the more isolated and private sphere of family.[57] Perhaps that is why Joanne Spillman, the last prioress of Swaffham Bulbeck, a small Benedictine house in the diocese of Ely, remained "in a cave on the grounds of the priory's vicarage" after this priory was closed.[58] Whether the ex-nuns of the diocese of Norwich continued their daily monastic routine is unknown, but their burial arrangements and testamentary bequests – gifts to high altars and requests for prayers for their souls and the souls of their friends, for example – indicate that despite their physical transition to secular life in post-

[54] NRO, Norwich Consistory Court 75 Wymer (1546); NRO, Norwich Consistory Court 75-77 Wymer (1546); NRO, Norwich Consistory Court, NRO 169 Punting (1545).

[55] Baskerville, "Married Clergy", p. 120 for the Shouldham nuns; NRO, Norwich Consistory Court 261 Hyll for Buttery.

[56] Roberta Gilchrist and Marilyn Oliva, *Religious Women in Medieval East Anglia* (Norwich, 1993), pp. 71-72.

[57] Barbara Harris, "A New Look at the Reformation: Aristocratic Women and Nunneries, 1450-1540", *Journal of British Studies* 32 (1993), 89-113 at p. 90; Warnicke, *Women of the English Renaissance*, pp. 84-85. Lyndal Roper, *The Holy Household: Women and Morals in Reformation Augsburg* (Oxford, 1989) discusses this aspect of the Reformation there.

[58] William Palmer, "The Benedictine Nunnery of Swaffham Bulbeck", *Proceedings of the Cambridge Antiquarian Society* 31 (1929), 30-65 at p. 35.

dissolution England, emotionally and psychologically they maintained their beliefs in the old faith.

The wills of ex-nuns indicate that at the very least these women remained in contact after their monasteries had been suppressed. In the diocese of Norwich both Elizabeth Dawney, last prioress of Blackborough, and Ela Buttery, Campsey Ash's last superior, bequeathed all of their worldly goods to women with whom they had lived as nuns.[59] Wills of ex-superiors and rank-and-file nuns from Yorkshire, London, and the county of Hampshire also frequently included bequests to women with whom they had previously lived and prayed.[60] Like their counterparts in the diocese of Norwich, these women demonstrated an abiding connection to each other in the face of incredible upheaval, a connection which speaks to the strength of their ties both as religious women and as friends in the temporal world.

Such commitments surely helped to mitigate the impact – both financial and psychological – of the nuns' conversion to secular life. Equally significant, however, sustained communal living arrangements also recall a long-standing tradition of informal religious communities of women identified in studies both of female monastic foundations and also of female recluses.[61] While most of these informal groupings were regularised by the Church hierarchy at some point, their existence throughout the Middle Ages and beyond suggests a strain of female piety which functioned outside of established Church parameters. And while the Church may not have recognised such informal groups of female religious, bequests to

[59] NRO, Norwich Consistory Court 47 Mayett (Dawney); NRO, Norwich Consistory Court 261 Hyll (Buttery).

[60] See, for example, Raine, *Wills and Inventories*, p. 193 for the will of Christianna Burgh, the last prioress of Nunkeeling, who made bequests to two of her fellow ex-nuns in her will dated 1566. This reference is also noted in Cross and Vickers, *Monks, Friars and Nuns*, pp. 532-33, and see *ibid.*, pp. 535-37, 544, 560-61, 584, 586, 588 for other examples; Paxton, "Nunneries of London", pp. 308-9.

[61] Sharon Elkins, *Holy Women of Twelfth-Century England* (Chapel Hill, 1988), pp. 48, 53, 71, 123.

them in the wills of local people demonstrate both a public acknowledgement of and support for these women.[62]

Significantly more women stayed living in community and in touch with each other for many, many years after the suppression of their convents than ex-male religious did, but this should not surprise.[63] Nuns' awards and pensions were significantly less than those the men received, and the male religious had many more options for employment especially in the new Church of England. But it would be wrong, I think, to explain the female religious' desire to stay together as simply financial expedience. Colin Richmond has suggested that the reformation of the Church in England was in part a de-feminisation of religion, that not only were female monasteries dissolved, but that "those means of religious expression particularly dear to women" were destroyed and expressly forbidden.[64] Such wholesale denuding of a religious culture must have compounded the difficulties of the nuns' transition to secular life. Given this cultural shift where expressions of female piety were not accommodated, these ex-nuns, like the women who had joined together in unregulated religious communities before them, established communities in order to satisfy spiritual or religious needs which were not being met by contemporary powers. Indeed, as mentioned before, these women's bequests to high altars and for intercessory prayers indicate that they very consciously maintained their beliefs in the old religion. Most, in fact, still referred to themselves as "good catholic" women or "honest catholic" women in pension lists of 1547 and 1553, times when such identification had ceased to mean very much. But while

[62] Information about the informal groups in the city of Norwich, for example, comes from the following wills: NRO, Norwich Consistory Court 102 Brosyerd (1458); PRO, Prerogative Court of Canterbury Probate 11/4/23 (1461); NRO, Norwich Consistory Court 30 Wylby (1444); these and more are listed in Gilchrist and Oliva, *Religious Women*, pp. 95-96. Norman Tanner, *The Church in Late Medieval Norwich* (Toronto, 1984), p. 203 noted two of the five settlements noted by myself and Gilchrist.

[63] Warnicke, *Women of the English Renaissance*, pp. 70-71.

[64] Colin Richmond, "The English Gentry and Religion, c. 1500", in Christopher Harper-Bill, ed., *Religious Belief and Ecclesiastical Careers in Late Medieval England* (Woodbridge, 1991), pp. 121-50 at pp. 140-42.

it may have been anachronistic to some people – perhaps most? – this identification clearly signified not only an abiding faith in the old religion, but also a tenacious self-perception of their status as religious women. Such self-identification combined with communal living arrangements undoubtedly provided a measure of stability to an otherwise unsafe passage to secular life.

Table 1

Ages of English Nuns at the Dissolution of the Monasteries

Years of Age	(No.)	%
15-20	(6)	4
21-30	(47)	28
31-40	(44)	27
41-50	(25)	15
51-60	(18)	10
61+	(25)	15
Totals	(165)	99

Table 2

Pensions Received by the Superiors of the Female Monasteries in the Diocese of Norwich Ranked According to Highest Amount

Name of Superior	Pension Received £	s	d	Monastery	Value in 1535 in £
Ela Buttery	23	6	8	Campsey Ash	182
Grace Sampson	13	6	8	Redlingfield	67
Cecily Suffield	8			Carrow	64
Elizabeth Wright	6	13	4	Flixton	23
Elizabeth Dawney	6			Blackborough	42
Barbara Mason	5			Marham	42
Elizabeth Fincham	5			Shouldham	138
Elizabeth Hoth	5			Thetford	38
Elizabeth Studfield	4			Crabhouse	24

Benedictine and Franciscan Cloisters: Partnership and Rivalry in the Thirteenth Century

Michael Robson

Saints Benedict and Francis, both natives of Umbria, are revered as the founders of two of the most influential religious orders in the western Church. The monk and the friar were intent on deeper communion with God through prayer and asceticism. While the former did this within the stability of the cloister, the latter was mobile, moving from one friary to another and pledged to a form of the apostolic life which featured preaching. The new and global dimensions of the friars' vocation were encapsulated in Francis' meeting with the allegorical Lady Poverty, who asked to see his cloister. He led her to a hill and showed her the whole world as far as she could see: that was his extensive friary.[1] The monastic world was part of the landscape of medieval Umbria and monks make fleeting appearances in the earliest biographies of Francis, occasionally as witnesses to his sanctity and miracles.[2] V. G. Green was not a solitary voice in his judgement that the monks bitterly

[1] S. Brufani, ed., *Sacrum commercium sancti Francisci cum domina Paupertate*, Medioevo Francescano, 1 (Assisi, 1990), pp. 170-73.

[2] Thomas of Celano, "Vita secundi S. Francisci", in *Analecta Franciscana*, 12 vols (Quaracchi, Florence, and then Grottaferrata, Rome, 1885-1983), 10:127-68 at p. 190, no. 101.

resented the friars' presence and ministry.[3] This study explores a sample of the areas in which monks and friars interacted, highlighting both tensions and collaboration.

Following Francis' clash with his father, he withdrew from Assisi and worked for several days as a scullion at the Benedictine monastery of San Verecundo near Gubbio. He wore a ragged shirt and was satisfied to be filled only with broth. He was not received with sympathy and was not even given an old garment. The reference to clothing is tantalisingly brief and Francis' first biographer does not make it clear whether he was taking temporary refuge there or whether he was toying with the idea of a monastic vocation. While no attempt is made to explain the unhappy ending to this visit, the phraseology does not altogether remove the suggestion that Francis had considered the idea of joining the community. Once his fame had begun to spread, the prior recalled the shabby treatment meted out to Francis and apologised, seeking pardon on behalf of himself and his monks.[4] Francis made other visits to this monastery, on whose behalf he later performed a miracle.[5] While he lived as a hermit and spent two years repairing ruined churches, it is unlikely that he did not give serious consideration to a monastic vocation, which offered an alternative lifestyle to the values of the market place. In the last twenty years of his life he remained attracted to the vocation of the hermit and enjoyed protracted spells of retreat.[6]

Disillusioned by the social divisions of his society, Francis turned increasingly towards God in search of an alternative vocation. After his decisive meeting with the leper in the plain below Assisi, he followed the traditional route of asceticism by

[3] V. G. Green, "The Franciscans in Medieval English Life (1224-1348)", *Franciscan Studies* 20 (1939), p. 103.

[4] Thomas of Celano, "Vita prima S. Francisci", in *Analecta Franciscana*, 10:1-117 at p. 15, no. 16.

[5] R. B. Brooke, ed. and trans., *The Writings of Leo, Rufino and Angelo, Companions of St Francis*, Oxford Medieval Texts (Oxford, repr. 1990), pp. 300-3, no. 7.

[6] C. H. Lawrence, *Medieval Monasticism: Forms of Religious Life in Western Europe in the Middle Ages*, 2nd edn (London, 1989), p. 246, draws attention to Francis' enduring interest in the eremetical ideal.

withdrawing from society. Did he regard the monasteries as too deeply entrenched in the economic structures to be places of resort for men and women with high ideals? Or was it the case that the ordered routine of the monastic life, with its different form of the apostolic life, did not appeal to him? When he visited Rome in 1209/10 to ask the blessing of Innocent III upon his fledgling fraternity, he was introduced to Cardinal John of St Paul, the reforming bishop of Santa Sabina, who urged him to follow a monastic rule.[7] This suggestion was firmly resisted on the grounds that Francis wanted to follow the Gospel to the letter and the monastic world did not satisfy all his aspirations. Eventually the cardinal abandoned his objections and agreed to present Francis' petition to the papal court, successfully championing the friars' cause. After discernment about whether the friars should live in cities or in remote places, Francis came to understand that they were sent to win souls for God.[8]

The lengthy interval between the initial papal approval of the Rule by Innocent III in 1209/10 and its formal confirmation by Honorius III on 29 November 1223 generated anxiety and insecurity among the friars, and Francis' absence in the Holy Land raised questions of authority within the nascent fraternity. On his return in 1220 an old question about Franciscan identity resurfaced during a general chapter attended by some 5,000 friars. Debate about the Rule was so wide-ranging that some friars were urging that the fraternity should adopt one of the traditional Rules. Advocates of this solution to the community's canonical standing pointed to the success being enjoyed by the Dominicans, who had adapted the Rule of St Augustine. They enlisted the services of Cardinal Ugolino, bishop of Ostia and the friars' protector, to persuade Francis to consider their recommendations. Francis patiently listened to this advice and then took the cardinal by the hand into the midst of the friars, categorically refusing to follow another Rule.

[7] For an examination of the Benedictine influence on another part of the Franciscan tradition see H. De Sainte-Marie, "Présence de la Règle bénédictine dans la Règle de sainte Claire", *Archivum Franciscanum Historicum*, 82 (1989), 3-20.

[8] Thomas of Celano, "Vita prima", pp. 25-28, nos 32-35.

He expostulated that God had shown him the way of humility and simplicity and indicated the course which he should take. No further consideration was given to the suggestion that Francis might choose to follow the Rules of Augustine, Bernard or Benedict.[9]

The Benedictines on Monte Subasio were among the friars' first benefactors. When the number of friars began to grow, Francis approached the abbot in search of a church for the friars' use. The abbot granted him the monastery's poorest church in the district of Assisi, Santa Maria degli Angeli, and expressed his wish that, should the fraternity expand, the chapel would remain the centre of the fraternity. Francis was overjoyed at the donation of the site and willingly agreed to the condition. Although the monastery had freely conceded the church to the friars, each year Francis sent a small wicker basket full of little fish to the monks; the friars took the fish to the monastery and in return received a jar full of oil. Traditional language informs the account given by the saint's companions, who note the piety of the abbot in granting the petition and the monks' co-operation with the will of God. The monks' gesture was interpreted as a significant act in the birth of the fraternity.[10] This was the first of many acts of monastic benevolence towards the friars throughout Christendom. Before 1229 the abbot and monks of St Cosmas in Trastevere at Rome gave the friars a hospice known as San Biagio.[11]

On 26 October 1231 Gregory of Naples, minister provincial of France, wrote to Odo, abbot of Saint-Denis in Paris, recalling the monks' hospitality during 1219: "when, as pilgrims we reached Saint-Denis, we had nothing and nowhere to lay our heads. You gave us lodging in a house which you owned".[12] The decision to dispatch a group of friars to England was taken in the early 1220s

[9] M. Bigaroni, ed., *Compilatio Assisiensis dagli Scritti di fra Leone e compagni su S. Francesco d'Assisi* (Assisi, 1992), chap. 18, pp. 56-59.

[10] Bigaroni, ed., *Compilatio Assisiensis*, chap. 56, pp. 126-47.

[11] L. Wadding, ed., *Annales Minorum seu Trium Ordinum a S. Francisco institutorum*, 32 vols, 3rd edn (Quaracchi, Florence, 1931-1964), 2:254.

[12] A. Callebaut, "Essai sur l'origine du premier couvent des Mineurs à Paris et sur l'influence de frère Grégoire de Naples", in *France Franciscaine*, 11 (1928), 5-30, 179-206 at pp. 9-10.

by Francis himself, who appointed Agnellus of Pisa as the leader of the mission. The initial party of nine friars seems to have assembled in northern France, perhaps at Paris, where Agnellus had been the *custos*. Mindful of the earlier hiccups accompanying the missions to France, Germany and Hungary, the friars set out in the late summer of 1224 and, on their way to the French coast, reached the priory of Holy Trinity at Fécamp, which had a priory at Cogges in Oxfordshire as well as other estates in England. They probably made use of the monks' knowledge of their estates in England and consulted them about plans for initial foundations there. The monks arranged for the friars' passage and may have supplied them with letters of introduction to monasteries. When the friars arrived on 10 September, they received Benedictine hospitality once again, spending two days at the cathedral priory of Christ Church in Canterbury.[13] Salimbene, the Franciscan chronicler who travelled widely in France and various provinces of Italy, was clearly not unaccustomed to monastic hospitality, proclaiming that he had dined with John of Piancarpino, the Franciscan papal legate, in friaries, abbeys and other places *non semel neque bis*. At Cluny, which he regarded as the most noble Benedictine monastery in Burgundy, he heard the monks contrasting the rapacious behaviour of papal legates with John's modest petition for a piece of cloth so that a tunic might be made for his *socius*.[14]

New religious orders did not always experience a smooth and gentle introduction to the ecclesiastical landscape and one reason for displays of antagonism by established communities was the threat which was posed to the vested interests of the regular and secular clergy. While the friars' clashes with the secular clergy have been well publicised, their more positive dealings with monastic communities have attracted less attention. Reports of the friars' appeals to the papacy and the texts of agreements which they made are not in short supply, as the pages of *Bullarium Franciscanum* and chronicles testify.

[13] Thomas of Eccleston, *Tractatus de adventu fratrum minorum in Angliam*, ed. A. G. Little (Manchester, 1951), pp. 3-8.

[14] Salimbene, *Salimbene de Adam, Cronica*, ed. G. Scalia, 2 vols, Scrittori d'Italia 232-33 (Bari, 1966), pp. 305-6.

The friars' activities at Vézélay, for example, aroused the monks' ire and relations deteriorated to the point where the monks took the law into their own hands. Gregory IX's letter of 3 June 1233 announced that he had received reports that the monks had destroyed and pillaged the friary; the abbot and monks were excommunicated for this act. Nonetheless, the monks and the friars reached an agreement, which Gregory described as an *amicabilis compositio*. The friars, whose numbers were increasing, were permitted to remain at Vézélay and celebrate the liturgy. A comparable new friary was to be constructed in place of the one which had been destroyed (*quae fuit per monachos diruta*). Nonetheless, steps were taken to safeguard monastic revenues and restrictions were placed upon the friars' liturgical activities: offerings on the altar during Mass were not to be received; tithes and other offerings were forbidden; the burial of lay people in their churches was proscribed. The abbot and convent were admonished not to expel the friars without the special licence of the pope. He then lifted the sentence of excommunication which he had delivered against the abbot and monks. On 8 June 1233 the pope wrote to the abbot and noted the terms of the agreement.[15]

The perception that the friars were attempting to extend their sphere of influence at the monks' expense lay behind more than one dispute. The friction between the abbey of St Martin and friars at Limoges in the 1240s is richly documented. The friars arrived there in 1223 and lodged initially at the church of St Paul. St Anthony of Padua arrived about two years later as the *custos* of the group of friaries in the area and in 1226 he transferred the friars from the original site to the land owned by the abbey of St Martin. Peter Coral, abbot of St Martin, reports that Anthony entered into an agreement whereby the friars settled on land belonging to the monastery, although certain agreements and conditions were imposed. Within a short time the friars wished to break free of the agreement and complained that the monks were holding to the original conditions. They began to build at an early date, between 1227 and 1242; a legal document of 26 May 1239 mentioned the

[15] *Bullarium Franciscanum*, ed. H. Sbaralea and C. Eubel, vols 1-7 (Rome and Quaracchi, Florence, 1759-1908), 1:110-12, nos 110, 111.

"ecclesia Fratrum Minorum prope Lemovicen". However, the monks complained that the friars had acted beyond their powers and obliged them to withdraw in 1243. On 21 January 1245 the pope wrote to the bishop of Angoulème, stating that John Pineta and some burgesses of the town had purchased land on the friars' behalf for the construction of a friary with the consent of the abbot and monastery, whose land it was. The name of Jesus was invoked by the monastic chronicler to emphasise that the monks were not at fault in this matter; blame was laid entirely at the friars' door.[16]

The question of burial in mendicant cemeteries quickly became one of the flash-points between the secular clergy and the friars, bedevilling their relations for much of the thirteenth century and culminating in Boniface VIII's *Super cathedram* on 18 February 1300. The same question impinged upon monastic communities which were accustomed to provide a resting place for their founders and benefactors. Within a decade of the death of St Francis, who had wished his followers to live in harmony with their clerical neighbours, some monasteries were showing signs of anxiety and irritation lest the friars begin the practice of burying lay people in their own churches. The embittered disputes of the later thirteenth century confirm that these fears were well grounded, although the friars were not always the guilty party. John Pecham, archbishop of Canterbury, compelled the monastic communities of Gloucester in 1285[17] and Worcester in 1290[18] to return bodies to the neighbouring Greyfriars for burial; in each case the deceased had expressed a wish for burial in the local friary. Nonetheless, although the great lords in thirteenth-century England were frequently benefactors to the mendicant orders, they rarely chose to be buried with them.[19]

[16] F. M. Delorme, "Les Cordeliers dans le Limousin aux XIIIe-XVe siècles", in *Archivum Franciscanum Historicum*, 32 (1939), 201-59 at pp. 215-22.

[17] John Pecham, *Registrum Epistolarum Fratris Ioannis Peckham*, ed. C. T. Martin, 3 vols, Rolls Series 77 (London, 1882-85), 3:905-6.

[18] H. R. Luard, ed., *Annales Monastici*, 4 vols, Rolls Series 36 (London, 1864-69), 4:499-504.

[19] B. Golding, "Burials and Benefactions: An Aspect of Monastic

While the friars were busy establishing themselves in Scotland, they aroused the suspicion and, in some cases, the opposition of the monastic orders. When they had marked out land for a cemetery at Roxburgh and requested its consecration by the Bishop of Glasgow, they came into conflict with the monks of Kelso. As patrons of all the burgh churches, the monks induced the secular clergy to protest about the consecration of the friars' cemetery. On 13 September 1235 the case was heard by William de Bondington, bishop of Glasgow, in the church of St Peter at Roxburgh. Herbert Mansuel, abbot of Kelso, and Martin, *custos* of the friars in Scotland, made their representations. The bishop gave his decision in the form of a restatement of the teaching of Gregory IX, granting the friars permission to bury their own dead in their churches and cemeteries. The friars were not allowed to bury lay people and the rights of the monks over their churches were to be safeguarded; that same afternoon the bishop proceeded with the consecration of the friars' church.[20]

The friars' sensitivity towards the rights and privileges of their monastic neighbours was exemplified by the promise of John of Piancarpino, minister provincial of Saxony, in 1237 to Abbot Conrad of Fulda that the friars would not preach on the special feast days of the monastery nor bury the abbey's servants in the Franciscan cemetery.[21] Agreements between the two orders were numerous and one of these bound the abbey of St Peter at Ghent and the friars in that city. Tensions had been raised by the friars' burial of Agnes, a parishioner of St John's, a parish within the monastery's jurisdiction. The monks protested that this action infringed their rights. Nonetheless, a *compositio* was drawn up, permitting the friars to bury four people from the abbey's jurisdiction in their

Patronage in Thirteenth-Century England", in *England in the Thirteenth Century: Proceedings of the 1984 Harlaxton Symposium*, ed. W. Ormrod (Nottingham, 1985), pp. 64-75 at p. 73.

[20] W. M. Bryce, *The Scottish Grey Friars*, 2 vols (Edinburgh, 1909), 1:6-7; 2:1-2.

[21] J. B. Freed, *The Friars and German Society in the Thirteenth Century* (Cambridge, Mass., 1977), p. 35; J. F. Schannat, *Diocesis Fuldensis cum annexa sua hierarchia* (Frankfurt am Main, 1727), no. 54.

cloisters each year with the consent of the monastery. The lengthy text, which indicates some experience in settling such demarcation disputes, also contained clauses for dealing with occasions when the monastery permitted fewer or more than four burials in the friary in any year. The agreement, reached in July 1252, was approved by the officials of the fraternity, beginning with the minister provincial in France, the *custos* of Flanders and the guardian of the local community. The document was then referred to the minister general at the general chapter of Metz in 1254.[22]

The network of monastic schools served as vital centres for the preservation and dissemination of the biblical, patristic and classical heritage in the early Middle Ages. It offered the best theological instruction to young men intent on study, and that conviction took the young St Anselm from Lombardy to Normandy in search of instruction from Lanfranc.[23] In the early twelfth century the leadership in theological studies passed to cathedral schools such as Laon. By the end of the century the schools of Paris were changing from cathedral schools to a university. The emergence of the new universities of Paris and Oxford, coincided with the birth of the mendicant movement, which produced the most influential theologians of the era, Albert the Great, Thomas Aquinas, Bonaventure and John Duns Scotus. The Benedictine heritage was deeply rooted and conspicuous in the early schools organised by the friars and immense respect was accorded to the Fathers of the Church, many of whom had lived the cloistered life. This interpretation draws support from the range of authorities cited by early Franciscan masters and Franciscan library catalogues, some of which survive from the fourteenth century. The prestige of Gregory the Great, for example, was such that he was hailed as the saint who excelled in teaching concerning morals.[24] The influence of

[22] M. Bihl, "De Capitulo Generali O. M. Metensi anno 1254 adsignando, deque antiquo sigillo Ministri Glis. (VIII illustr.)", *Archivum Franciscanum Historicum*, 4 (1911), 425-35 at pp. 428-30.

[23] R. W. Southern, ed. and transl., *The Life of St Anselm Archbishop of Canterbury by Eadmer* (Oxford, 1962), pp. 8-10.

[24] Bonaventure, "De reductione artium ad theologiam", in *Doctoris Seraphici S. Bonaventurae Opera Omnia*, 10 vols (Quaracchi, Florence, 1882-

Benedictine authors such as William, abbot of Saint-Thierry, who subsequently joined the Cistercians,[25] and St Anselm, abbot of Bec, on the early Franciscan school has been demonstrated by J. G. Bougerol.[26] Anselm's guidance and authority on soteriological questions were amply demonstrated in Alexander of Hales' *Summa Theologica*, where the question *Utrum humana natura possit reparari sine satisfactione peccati per quod lapsa est*[27] consists of a mosaic of quotations from the *Cur Deus homo*.[28]

By the middle of the thirteenth century the reputation of the friars' schools was rising and some of them were opening their doors to non-friars. In 1248 an exiled Benedictine bishop of Corsica was accustomed to attend daily Mass and the lectures in theology given by Stephen, an English friar in Genoa.[29] So secure had the mendicant ascendance in theological studies become that some monasteries decided to apply to the friars to secure the services of theologians. Between 1275 and 1314 three successive friars taught at the cathedral priory of Christ Church in Canterbury. It was only when the monks had trained their own masters that they no longer required the friars' services.[30] The mendicants' impact on the medieval Church and their influential position in the new universities conferred great benefits upon them, not least in recruitment. They did not require students to turn their backs on the world of theological studies and were beginning to attract young men who, in an earlier age, might have chosen the monastic life. By

1902), 5:319-325 at p. 321.

[25] J. G. Bougerol, "Saint Bonaventure et Guillaume de Saint-Thierry", *Antonianum*, 46 (1971), 298-321.

[26] See his "Saint Bonaventure et saint Anselme", *Antonianum*, 47 (1972), 333-61.

[27] Alexander of Hales, *Summa Theologica*, 6 vols (Quaracchi, Florence and Grottaferrata, Rome, 1924-79), 4:14-17, caput 4, which is translated as "whether human nature could be restored without satisfaction for the sin by which it fell".

[28] Anselm, *S. Anselmi Cantuariensis Archiepiscopi Opera Omnia*, ed. F. S. Schmitt, 6 vols (Edinburgh, 1946-61), 2:38-133.

[29] Salimbene, *Cronica*, pp. 460-61.

[30] M. Robson, "Franciscan Lectors at Christ Church Cathedral Priory, Canterbury, 1275-1314", *Archaeologia Cantiana*, 112 (1993), 261-81.

the 1230s, however, there is evidence that the friars were not only beginning to feel more confident about their academic abilities, but they were also talking disdainfully about other religious. In their dispute with the Cistercians at Scarborough the friars poured scorn on the learning of the monastic orders.[31] In 1249 such mendicant contempt prompted the Cistercians to follow the example of the Benedictines and obtain papal permission to build a school at Paris.[32]

The emergence of new religious orders was not invariably accompanied by a boom in new buildings, and some churches and conventual buildings of older orders were transferred to the newer ones. One of the best known churches which the friars received from the Benedictines was the basilica of Santa Maria in Aracoeli in Rome. The friars had complained about the bad conditions in which they lived at Trastevere, where, among other things, the quality of the air was poor. In 1248 they approached the papal court for help. On 12 July 1249 Innocent IV wrote to Raynaldo dei Conti di Segni, the friars' cardinal protector, arranging to have them installed in the monastic buildings. The monks, despite their protests, were dispersed and the monastery with its gardens, ecclesiastical ornaments and manuscripts was granted to the friars.[33] The Benedictine church Santa Maria Maggiore at Tivoli, served by only four or five monks, was granted to the friars in 1241, although they did not take possession until 1256. In late 1258 the friars received some monks for a light meal (*collatio*), but before taking their leave the monks helped themselves to books and church furnishings from the friary. On 2 December 1258 Alexander IV commanded the bishop of Tivoli to compel the monks to restore the items.[34] The disgruntled monks may have felt justified in reclaiming their own possessions.

[31] Matthew Paris, *Matthei Parisiensis, Monachi Sancti Albani Chronica Majora*, ed. H. R. Luard, 7 vols, Rolls Series 77 (London, 1872-83), 4:280.

[32] Matthew Paris, *Chronica*, 5:79-80.

[33] *Bullarium Franciscanum,* 1:521-22, 530-31, 556-57, 616-17, nos 288, 304, 346, 418; *Annales Minorum*, 3:285-312.

[34] *Bullarium Franciscanum epitome et supplementum* (Quaracchi, Florence, 1908), p. 100, no. 1015; *Annales Minorum*, 3:72, 468; 4:50-51, 492, 496-98.

The new reform movements of the Middle Ages attracted young men from various parts of the Church, including those who had already been professed as religious. The friars made a similar impact and their early years were marked by the arrival of distinguished ecclesiastics as well as scholars. The monks and abbot of the Benedictine community at Antioch embraced the Franciscan fraternity between 1220 and 1230.[35] As abbot of St Mary in Stade, a Benedictine monastery, Albert of Stade, had made a vain attempt to persuade his monastery to embrace the Cistercian reform. His interest in reformed religious life eventually prompted him to take the Franciscan habit at Stade in 1240. In the same year he was writing his chronicle, which he later continued, the first general chronicle to be written by a Franciscan, the *Annales Stadenses*.[36] Benedict d'Alignan entered the Benedictines, attaining the office of abbot. He was subsequently elected as bishop of Marseilles, resigning in 1267 to become a friar and bringing his collection of manuscripts to the fraternity. He was clothed on the feast of St Benedict and lived humbly and laudably until his death in 1277. He was buried in a stone vault in the Franciscan church at Marseilles, where miracles were worked.[37]

While there were numerous distinguished recruits to the fraternity, by the middle of the thirteenth century some discontented friars decided to become Benedictines. Guidolino of Ferrara left the friars for the monastery of Nonantola in the diocese of Modena, where his conduct so impressed all the monks that he was chosen as their abbot. This caused a great quarrel between the monks and the friars when John Gaetano was the latter's cardinal protector. The friars used their influence to prevent Guidolino from taking up the abbatial office, although the monks spent 10,000 imperial pounds in

[35] G. Golubovich, *Biblioteca Bio-Bibliografica della Terra Santa e dell'oriente francescano, 1 (1215-1300)* (Quaracchi, Florence, 1906), pp. 66, 68-70.

[36] Freed, *Friars and German Society*, pp. 114, 121; A. G. Little, *Franciscan Papers, Lists, and Documents* (Manchester, 1943), p. 33.

[37] Salimbene, *Cronica*, pp. 806-7; W. R. Thomson, *Friars in the Cathedral: The First Franciscan Bishops 1226-1261*, Pontifical Institute of Mediaeval Studies, Studies and Texts 33 (Toronto, 1975), pp. 212-17.

the case. When they saw that they were labouring in vain, they refused to elect another abbot, but instead made Guidolino lord of the abbey, so that he was as good as abbot. Salimbene, a confrère and friend of the future abbot at the friary in Ravenna, remarked that Guidolino was always glad to see the friars and receive them at Nonantola. He petitioned the fraternity to keep two scribes in that place at the monastery's own expense in order to make abundant copies of the books in their library on the acts of the saints for the friars.[38]

The polemical literature of the thirteenth century provided a forum for an explication of the mendicant ideal, including some comparisons between the Benedictines and the Franciscans. Salimbene contrasted the government of his own order with that of the monastic orders. He believed that the preservation of a religious order required a frequent change of leaders, advancing three reasons for this. First, leaders who are in power for a long time become insolent, as is apparent in the abbots, who remain in office for life. As a result they treat their subordinates badly and hold them to be worth no more than the fifth wheel of a wagon, which is nothing. Abbots eat meat with secular men, while the monks in the refectory eat vegetables; they behave towards their subordinates in a niggardly and unseemly manner, whereas they themselves choose to live lavishly and in almost complete freedom.[39] A certain amount of criticism of the monastic orders is found in John Pecham's writings in defence of his order.[40] Monastic libraries preserved William of St Amour's attacks on the friars and such criticisms were quoted with approval by monastic writers in fourteenth-century England.[41]

Bonaventure's lengthy question concerning mendicancy contains numerous references to monastic practice and the evolution

[38] Salimbene, *Cronica*, pp. 909-10; *Bullarium Franciscanum*, 3:343; 4:20.

[39] Salimbene, *Cronica*, p. 159.

[40] John Pecham, *Fratris Johannis Pecham quondam archiepiscopi Cantuariensis Tractatus tres de Paupertate*, ed. C. L. Kingsford, A. G. Little and F. Tocco, British Society of Franciscan Studies, 2 (Aberdeen, 1910), pp. 167, 169, 174.

[41] P. R. Szittya, *The Antifraternal Tradition in Medieval Literature* (Princeton, 1986), pp. 99-106.

of the friars' vocation.[42] While many regarded the Franciscans as reviving the conditions of the apostolic Church, their critics accused Saints Francis and Dominic of the novelty of mendicancy.[43] These claims were firmly rejected by Bonaventure, who located the friars within the mainstream of the history of religious life. Dominic issued a posthumous curse on those who wished to introduce possessions into the order and Francis was accustomed to seek alms, a practice which was approved by the working of miracles.[44] St Benedict had been supported by alms.[45] Bonaventure maintained that those who wished to impugn this form of life reprove not only the *ordo pauperum*, but also the pope, who approved its Rule, and the great assembly of the saints who begged: Francis, Dominic and Benedict, plus the ranks of the prophets and apostles; even Jesus Christ was poor and a beggar. In short, the Gospels speak of Jesus' example in seeking alms and recommending his apostles to do the same.[46] In defending the friars' dependence upon alms, Bonaventure commented that monasticism too, was established upon alms[47] and that evangelical poverty was a particularly cogent support to the friars' proclamation of the Gospel.[48]

St Francis' espousal of evangelical poverty was interpreted by Bonaventure as a providential antidote to a twofold problem afflicting both society and the Church: the greed of the new urban centres and clerical avarice. Mendicant preaching was regarded as combating the vice of avarice. In the early Church the apostles and their disciples extirpated idolatry and in the intermediate period men, steeped in an appropriate interpretation of the Scriptures, eradicated heresy. In the medieval period God raised up the friars, who voluntarily embraced evangelical poverty and mendicancy, to rout avarice. Bonaventure argued that the friars had a divinely

[42] Bonaventure, "Quaestiones disputatae de perfectione evangelica", in *Opera Omnia*, 5:117-98 at pp. 134-55.

[43] *Ibid.*, no. 20, p. 136.

[44] *Ibid.*, *contra*, nos 22-23, pp. 138-39.

[45] *Ibid.*, *sed contra*, nos 20-21, p. 138.

[46] *Ibid.*, *conclusio*, pp. 141-42.

[47] *Ibid.*, *resplicatio adversus obiectiones postea factas*, no. V, p. 155.

[48] *Ibid.*, *conclusio*, p. 141.

commissioned role in the history of the Church and he vigorously defended the fraternity's special heritage. He maintained that voluntary poverty was the foundation and perfection of the Gospel, which had flourished in the beginning of the Church.[49]

The friars' activities impinged on the jurisdiction and income of monastic churches and feelings ran high; in some instances the friars were obliged to withdraw from monastic towns. Some sermons were delivered with the intention of increasing the monks' tolerance towards the mendicants.[50] There is ample evidence that agreements were reached on points of tension and monks were frequently generous to the friars. In 1255, for example, John of Parma, minister general, thanked the abbot of Saint-Vincent at Ghent for his devotion and kindness to the friars.[51] On occasion the monks invited the friars to preach in their churches and to teach theology in their cloisters; sometimes friars were appointed as confessors to Benedictine communities of women,[52] on episcopal advice.[53] On 9 October 1260 Robert, minister provincial of France, extended the friars' spiritual benefits to the abbot and monastery of Saint-Martin at Tournai.[54] In the early period between 1225 and 1300 Benedictine communities could have been forgiven for regarding their Franciscan neighbours with that mixture of irritation

[49] *Ibid., conclusio, ad obiecta,* no. 20, pp. 147-48.

[50] P. Gratien, "Sermons franciscains du Cardinal Eudes de Châteauroux (+1273)", in *Études Franciscaines*, 29 (1913), 171-95, 647-55, at pp. 188-95.

[51] U. d'Alençon, "Thomas d'Eccleston, ses nouveaux éditeurs et le chapitre général de Metz", in *Études Franciscaines*, 23 (1910), 95-99, at pp. 97-98.

[52] A. G. Little, *Studies in English Franciscan History* (Manchester, 1917), p. 119, note 1, shows that Franciscans were either licensed or recommended as confessors to Augustinian, Benedictine and Cistercian communities of women.

[53] *Registrum Peckham*, 3:845-51. In 1279 Pecham envisaged that the nuns at Godstow would engage two or four Dominicans and Franciscans as confessors. From the end of the thirteenth century the episcopal registers in England contain numerous licences for friars to serve as confessors to Benedictine nuns.

[54] A. Callebaut, "Lettres Franciscaines concernant la Belgique et la France au XIIIe-XIVe", *Archivum Franciscanum Historicum*, 7 (1914), 247-63, at pp. 254-55.

and jealousy sometimes experienced by an older brother towards a younger one.

Rhineland Dominicans, Meister Eckhart and the Sect of the Free Spirit

Walter Senner

In his commentary on the Dominican constitutions Humbert of Romans (d. 1277) explains that the defence of the Catholic faith against heresies has to be regarded as the principal motive for the foundation of this religious order, and preaching as its principal activity to achieve this end.[1] The aim of this paper is to investigate how Rhineland Dominicans dealt with the new spiritual movements comprising, among others, Beguines, Beghards and, especially, the so called sect of the Free Spirit.

Beguines usually settled near Franciscan and Dominican convents in order to benefit from the spiritual direction of the friars;[2] their first appearance in Germany was at Cologne about 1223.[3] Their male counterparts, the Beghards, were fewer in number but in Cologne they formed two convents, one of which was to join the third order of the Franciscans in 1329. The other one, called Lungenkonvent, chose Rutger Overstolz, one of the most renowned

[1] B. M. Reichert, ed., *Humbertus de Romanis, Opera de Vita Regulari*, 2 vols (Taurini, 1902), 2:38, no. 12.

[2] J. Asen, "Die Beginen in Köln", in *Zahlreich wie die Sterne des Himmels*, Bensberger Protokolle, 70 (Bergisch Gladbach, 1992), p. 144; *Regesten der Erzbischöfe von Köln im Mittelalter*, 11 vols (Bonn and elsewhere, 1901-92) vol. 3, no. 2161.

[3] Asen, "Beginen", pp. 135-70.

citizens as procurator in 1326.[4] As early as 1247 there were reports of conflicts between parish priests and Beguines in Cologne because the secular clergy were trying to exact a special contribution from them and to break their links with the mendicant orders.[5] In 1307 the diocesan synod excommunicated the *Beggardi et Beggarde et Apostoli* on the strength of their heretical views.[6] The list of charges is incoherent; it contains, among other things, the accusation that their way alone led to salvation, and that a husband could leave his wife without her consent in obedience to God.[7] The ecumenical council of Vienne in 1311-1312 sharply criticised both the Beghards and the Beguines who were living like religious but not obeying a recognised rule. By speculating on the divine Trinity, it was stated, they led many simple people into error. Their communities were to be prohibited and their members and supporters excommunicated.[8] The main accusations centred on their belief in the possibility of attaining perfection in this life and, in that state once achieved, the freedom from all restraint in any sphere of action.[9] The Cologne diocesan synod of 1319 repeated the condemnation against them and also denounced all Dominicans, Franciscans and the other mendicants for their support of the Beguines.[10]

Several chronicles of Cologne of the 1320s and 1330s describe heresy taking root in the city at this time, and the archbishop appointed a commission including Franciscans and Dominicans to

[4] H. Johag, *Die Beziehungen zwischen Klerus und Burgerschaft in Köln zwischen 1250 und 1350*, Rheinisches Archiv, 103 (Bonn, 1965), pp. 101ff.

[5] Asen, "Beginen", p. 103.

[6] *Regesten der Erzbischöfe*, 4:229.

[7] J. de Guibert, ed., *Documenta Ecclesiastica Christianae Perfectionis Studium Spectantia* (Rome, 1931), p. 154.

[8] G. Alberigo, ed., *Conciliorum Oecumenicorum Decreta* (Bologna, 1973), p. 374, no. 16.

[9] H. Denzinger, ed., *Enchiridium Symbolorum Definitionum et Declarationum de Rebus Fidei et Morum* (Freiburg im Breisgau, 1991), nos 831-33.

[10] H. Lepper, "Unbekannte Synodalstatuten der Kölner Erzbischöfe Heinrich von Virneburg und Wilhelm von Gennep", *Annuarium Historiae Conciliorum*, 11 (1979), 354.

investigate the adherents.[11] As a result some of the lapsed were brought back to the true faith, but two priests, one layman and six women persevered in their errors. Walter, their leader, was burnt alive while the others were handed over to perpetual imprisonment.[12]

From the remaining sources we do not learn anything about their doctrine. However, the details of the so called sect of the Free Spirit in Cologne have come to light in the minutes of an inquisition concerning one of its members, Johannes de Brunis (or Bruns), a shoemaker from Brno in Moravia.[13] After hearing about the "perfect life" of the Beghards in Cologne he had left his wife against her will and made his way to join their community in the southern part of the city, where he was received by a master Nicholas. He progressed over the next two decades to become one of the inner circle of the perfect until, eventually, remorse overtook him and he left to join the Dominicans as a lay brother. The minutes of the inquisition are preserved at Greifswald;[14] they record the testimony of de Brunis, which is to be regarded as trustworthy, and it is important in being the most detailed and explicit surviving evidence for this underground movement.[15] Wilhelm Janssen and Robert E. Lerner

[11] For the complex background see also F. J. Schmale, *Deutschlands Geschichtsquellen im Mittelalter* (Darmstadt, 1976), 1:105-12, 353-69. As to the differing accounts of the events described here see W. Senner, "Meister Eckhart in Köln", in *Meister Eckhart: Lebensstationen-Redesituationen*, ed. K. Jacobi (Berlin, 1997), pp. 205-35 at pp. 220-22.

[12] G. Waitz, ed., *Chronica Regia Coloniensis cum Continuationibus* in MGH, Scriptores Rerum Germanicarum, 18 (1880), p. 363.

[13] W. Wattenbach, ed., *Über die Secte der Brüder vom Freien Geiste*, Sitzungsberichte der Kgl. Preuss, Akademie der Wissenschaften, Phil.-Hist. Klasse 29 (1887), pp. 529-37.

[14] Wattenbach, *Über die Secte*, pp. 527-28. The manuscript was formerly in the library of the Dominican priory in Greifswald but is now in the Evangelisches Konsistorium there.

[15] Wattenbach, *Über die Secte*, p. 528. R. E. Lerner is sceptical about this record and suspects clerical prejudice behind it; see *The Heresy of the Free Spirit in the Later Middle Ages* (Berkeley, 1972), pp. 108-12. On the other hand, in his *Heresy in the Later Middle Ages* (Manchester, 1967), 1:371-77, G. Leff accepts the testimonies of the witnesses. Some historians doubt that this sect

place de Brunis in the Lungenkonvent but according to the record it must have been another community, *prope S. Stephanum* (i.e., in the south of Cologne), not named by the Cologne sources. The latter are almost entirely concerned with legal transactions relating to properties, transactions with which these espousers of radical religious views and of poverty would have had no truck.[16]

The simple members of their group observed the rule of poverty in all its strictness as the testimony of Nicholas makes clear:

> "Brother, when you want to remain with us you have to give everything into our hands ... When you appear in front of the brothers you will deposit everything before them on the table ... the true follower does not have any property but is as naked of all material goods as Christ on the cross".[17]

De Brunis' deposition continues:

> And when I stood there naked they permitted me to wear a shirt [made] out of a hundred patches, and they said "with this shirt you shall be vested, as Christ was vested with jeering and contempt. For the sake of Christ you shall endure the contempt of all men patiently ... if, tomorrow, when you are going through town, someone calls you a heretic and beats you up or harasses you in some other way, you shall not answer him but sustain everything patiently".

The purpose of severe mortification was to lead to personal liberty,

ever actually existed: see A. Vauchez in *Geschichte des Christentums*, vol. 6 of *Die Zeit der Zerreissproben* (Freiburg im Breisgau, 1991), p. 316, and R. N. Swanson, "Literacy, Heresy, History and Orthodoxy: Perspectives and Permutations for the Later Middle Ages", in *Heresy and Literacy 1000-1530*, ed. P. Biller (Cambridge, 1994), pp. 279-93 at p. 281.

[16] W. Janssen, *Das Erzbistum Köln im späten Mittelalter*, Geschichte des Erzbistums Köln, 2, pt 1 (Cologne, 1995), p. 600, but Johag, *Beziehungen*, p. 101.

[17] Wattenbach, *Über die Secte*, p. 529.

> "so that your worldly self may be diminished, annihilated and finally subdued entirely to the spirit ... your [human] nature has to be broken and subdued to the divine will so that it will obey it and be entitled to any action it desires".[18]

The perfect however, having become free, as distinct from the simple members, were no longer bound by rules:

> "Now you have reached everything belonging to the state of poverty ... your outward nature that has been consumed in the service of Christ now needs to be restored for that service ... eat as often as it pleases you ... [and] do not confess that to the priests".[19]

In opposition to the formal authority of the church those who were "free in the spirit" claimed a charismatic authority:

> ... a brother free in the spirit can preach to the people ... and when he will be asked who authorises his preaching he will answer: "if people can hear the truth and learn it, they can receive it from me just as well as from a priest ... because the poor of Christ draw truth out of the abyss of the Trinity ... [even without] being able to read and not knowing Holy Scripture".[20]

This perfect liberty of spirit which sanctions all that man's nature may desire leads to unification with God:

> In the same way the brothers who live in the spirit, once they have come to the perfect state of liberty, are transformed so completely that they are made one with God, and God completely and bodily [one] with them.[21]

Without making any reference to the Free Spirit, Kurt Ruh has observed that among German Dominicans at the beginning of the

[18] *Ibid.*, p. 532.
[19] *Ibid.*
[20] *Ibid.*, p. 533.
[21] *Ibid.*

fourteenth century there was a "host of preachers",[22] some of whose sermons survive to reveal how they approached the sect and its doctrines. In the remainder of this paper I shall limit myself to a brief account of three of the less well known friars and their sermons and also to Meister Eckhart.

Nicholas de Argentina, the first of the three, comes to our notice in Basel in 1318; after studies in Paris he came to Cologne in 1323 as lector in the Dominican *studium generale*. It was he who, as papal visitator and vicar, investigated the charges against Eckhart and defended him.[23] In his sermons he provided a practical guide for the way leading to perfection based on five actions of outward behaviour and five of inward behaviour. These bear similarities to the teachings of the sect of the Free Spirit with regard to the necessity for humiliation. However, they contain no criticism of sacramental and other orthodox practices and the importance of frequent, honest confession is stressed.[24]

In a sermon on Dives and Lazarus Nicholas contrasts God's mercy with the mercilessness of the rich, without any reference to the value of poverty. He not only recommends humility and trust in God in the face of hatred and rejection but requires the faithful to root out pride and not to despise the condemned. He also encourages prayers to win indulgences for the poor souls in purgatory.[25] His so called "sermon of the golden mountain", dating from the period of his lectorship at Cologne, stresses the importance

[22] K. Ruh, *Geschichte der abendländischen Mystik* (vol. 3 of *Die Mystik des deutschen Predigerorens und ihre Grundlegung durch die Hochscholastik*) (Munich, 1995), p. 389.

[23] T. Kaeppeli, *Scriptores Ordinis Praedicatorum Medii Aevi*, 3 vols (Rome, 1980), 3:143-45; K. Ruh, ed., *Verfasserlexikon der Deutschen Literatur des Mittelalters* (Berlin, 1987), 6, cols 1153-62 (article by E. Hillenbrand and K. Ruh).

[24] K. Bihlmeyer, "Kleine Beiträge zur Geschichte des deutschen Mystik", in *Beiträge zur Geschichte der Renaissance und Reformation*, ed. L. Fischer et al. (Munich, 1917), pp. 45-62 at pp. 46-48.

[25] F. Pfeiffer, *Deutsche Mystiker des vierzhennten Jahrhunderts* (Göttingen, 1845), 1:264-69, 270, 277, 283.

of continued repentance in the spiritual life.[26] All of these can be presumed as having been addressed to congregations which included adherents of the Free Spirit.

A second friar, John der Fûterer, from Strasbourg was a friend of Henry Suso who was greatly influenced by Eckhart's teaching.[27] In one of his sermons Fûterer includes among the people of whom God disapproves, "those who are poor and haughty".[28] When we regard the self-understanding of the *perfecti* of the Free Spirit, I suggest that it is probable these remarks refer to them.

John de Sterngassen (born c. 1285) is the third of the friars under consideration. He was lector in Strasbourg in 1316 during Eckhart's stay there and he may have been lector in Cologne in 1333.[29] In his sermons, which resemble some of Eckhart's but with a more popular appeal, the doctrines of the Free Spirit do not appear directly, but from the treatment of parallel themes his position can be inferred. Wealth, for example, cannot make man truly happy, as concern over possessions becomes preoccupation filled with anxiety and unrest. This is a functional view, very much like that of Thomas Aquinas on religious poverty.[30] *Luterkeit*, an untranslatable term rendered inadequately as "purity", is a constant theme in Sterngassen who explains its relation to freedom by means of a metaphor: in the "country of freedom" lies the "city of purity".[31] The complete union of the soul with God is expressed by him as identity, an identity not in essence but in vision.[32] Grace, which is received

[26] J. Konig, ed., "Die Chronik der Anna von Munzingen", *Freiburger Diozesan-Archiv*, 13 (1880), 129-236, especially p. 192.

[27] K. Bihlmeyer, ed., *Heinrich Seuse, Deutsche Schriften* (Stuttgart, 1907), *Vita*, chap. 6.

[28] Bihlmeyer, "Kleine Beiträge", pp. 50-52, especially p. 51.

[29] W. Senner, *Johannes von Sterngassen und sein Sentzenkommentar*, Quellen und Forschungen zur Geschichte des Dominikanerordens, new ser. 4-5, 2 vols (Berlin, 1995), 1:167-68.

[30] Senner, *Sterngassen*, 2:362. For Aquinas' view on poverty see U. Horst, *Evangelische Armut und Kirche*, Quellen und Forschungen zur Geschichte des Dominikanerordens, new ser. 1 (Berlin, 1992), pp. 29-13 2.

[31] Senner, *Sterngassen*, 2:349, 23-32.

[32] Senner, *Sterngassen*, 2:352.

from God in *luterkeit*, is necessary for salvation;[33] repentance is recommended as helpful even in the state of mortal sin.[34]

It has been taken for granted that Meister Eckhart directed the Cologne Dominicans' *studium generale* in the 1320s, despite the lack of any supporting evidence. This assumption has diverted the attention of scholars from what he actually did in Cologne. In Strasbourg he had been commissioned by the Dominican master general for the *cura monialium*. This was a difficult task in an atmosphere in which Beguines were persecuted and other spirituals were under suspicion.[35] After he had successfully resolved the problems there Eckhart came to Cologne and proceeded, through his preaching, to deal with a similar situation in this city.[36]

A number of explicit references in his German sermons show that many were delivered in Cologne churches, especially in those of the convents of Benedictine and Cistercian nuns.[37] Through a careful analysis of the sermons Joachim Theisen has found that Eckhart prepared them with the Dominican missal at hand and always in mind.[38] This is of particular interest because of the references to specific days in the liturgical year which can be dated with a fair degree of certainty. Ten sermons, for example, have been convincingly dated by Theisen in Lent 1326 and they must have been preached, therefore, in Cologne during the time of Eckhart's trial.[39] Others, quoted in the "Rechtfertigungschrift" or "Defence", were probably delivered between 8 September and 7 October of the previous year.[40]

[33] Senner, *Sterngassen*, 2:352.

[34] Senner, *Sterngassen*, 2:365, 373, 374. Sterngassen, however, does not follow Eckhart's view that *opera mortua*, committed in the state of mortal sin, can become meritorious after repentance, *ibid.*, 2:333.

[35] A. Patschovsky, "Strassburger Beginenverfolgungen im 14 Jahrhundert", *Deutsches Archiv zur Erforschung des Mittelalters*, 30 (1974), 56-198.

[36] Senner, "Meister Eckhart", pp. 205-35.

[37] Meister Eckhart, *Deutsche Werke*, ed. J. Quint (Stuttgart, 1958-), Sermons 13-15, 22.

[38] J. Theisen, *Predigt und Gottesdienst* (Frankfurt am Main, 1990).

[39] Theisen, *Predigt und Gottesdienst*, p. 121.

[40] Theisen, *Predigt und Gottesdienst*, p. 122.

Modern historians are not the first to link Eckhart with the brothers and sisters of the Free Spirit.[41] His earlier Erfurt sermons had aroused the suspicion of the Augustinian Henry de Friemar the elder.[42] Also, the Franciscan minister general, Michael de Cesena, who denied the accusations of heresy against himself, pointed his finger at Eckhart as an example of a real heretic.[43] Jan van Ruysbroeck (1293-1381), even described Eckhart as the founding father of the sect of the Free Spirit.[44]

Against the sect's practices of extreme austerity required at the beginning and the achievement of perfection attained by this way, Eckhart stresses the importance of reason, not only as the source of knowledge but also as the medium for unification with God:

> Will and love fall on God as being good, and if He were not good, they would ignore Him. Intellect penetrates right up into the essence without heeding [literally, even before thinking of] goodness or power or wisdom or whatever is accidental. It does not care what is added [literally, what is ascribed] to God, it takes Him in Himself, sinks into the essence, and takes God as He is pure essence.[45]

The *seelenfünklein, scintilla animae* or spark of intellect, is in this context "none other than a tiny spark of the divine nature, a divine light, a ray, and an imprint of the divine nature".[46] For

[41] See, for example, H. C. Lea, *A History of the Inquisition of the Middle Ages*, 3 vols (New York, repr. 1956), 1:360-62.

[42] A. Zumkeller, *Ein Zeitgenosse Eckeharts zu Fehlentwicklungen in der damaligen mystischen Bewegung, Würzburger Diözesan-Geschichtsblätter* (1975), pp. 229-38.

[43] See his *Appellatio maior* in M. Laurent, "Autour du Procès de Maître Eckhart", *Divus Thomas* [Piacenza], 13 (1936), pp. 446-47.

[44] C. de Vooys, "Meister Eckart en de nederlandse mystiek", *Nederlandsch archief voor kerkgeschiedenis*, new ser. 3 (1905), p. 192.

[45] Sermon 37 in *Deutsche Werke*, ed. Quint, 2:216 and an English translation in *Meister Eckhart: German Sermons and Treatises*, ed. M. Walshe, 2 vols (London, 1979-81), 1:230.

[46] *Deutsche Werke*, ed. Quint, 2:211; *German Sermons*, ed. Walshe, 1:229.

Eckhart, it is not the result of human ascetic endeavour or perfection but of divine grace which carries the soul beyond the limitations of the finite and leads to the union of man with God as a permanent, not merely a transitory, spiritual experience.[47] This spiritual experience is simple and can be experienced by all, but it cannot be induced: "whoever shall hear the eternal wisdom of the Father must be within, must be at home, and must be one".[48]

What matters for Eckhart is not subjective spiritual experience; it is, rather, the deepest dimension of reality, the presence in man of the Son in whom the Father reveals everything.[49] To be aware of this, man must come out of his self-containment in order to become the Son. "Such a person stays in God's knowing and in God's love and becomes nothing other than what God is Himself".[50] There is no method for this, no instrument, although Eckhart stresses the abandonment of self which may lead on to "the noblest and the ultimate thing that a person can forsake [and that] is that he forsakes God for God's sake".[51] The decisive difference between Eckhart and the Free Spirit lies in the view of man and his destiny:

> [That] Nature, which is from God, seeks nothing outside of itself: indeed nature, as it is in itself, has nothing to do with colour. For nature, which is of God, seeks nothing else but God's likeness.[52]

[47] *Deutsche Werke*, ed. Quint, 2:212, 219; cf. Sermon 33 at 2:152-54, and Sermon 26 at 2:24-25.

[48] Sermon 12 in *Deutsche Werke*, ed. Quint, 1:193; an English translation is in *Meister Eckhart: Teacher and Preacher*, ed. B. McGinn (New York, 1986), p. 267.

[49] *Deutsche Werke*, ed. Quint, 1:193; *Meister Eckhart*, ed. McGinn, p. 267.

[50] *Deutsche Werke*, ed. Quint, 1:194; *Meister Eckhart*, ed. McGinn, p. 267.

[51] *Deutsche Werke*, ed. Quint, 1:196; *Meister Eckhart*, ed. McGinn, p. 268.

[52] Sermon 51 in *Deutsche Werke*, ed. Quint, 2:471; English translation in *German Sermons*, ed. Walshe, 2:251ff. Walshe's translation "nothing to do with outward appearances" is a misunderstanding. For Eckhart's generalisation of Aristotle's theorem that, in order to perceive objects, the eye must be devoid of

Eckhart discusses the ethical views of the Free Spirit movement in an Ascension sermon which, perhaps, may not belong to the Cologne corpus.[53] First, he takes up the basic intention of the Free Spirit and responds: "God does not force the will but places it in freedom in such a way that it wills nothing but what God himself is and what freedom itself is".[54] Then he proceeds to expound his understanding of the meaning of freedom that is in sharp contrast to the libertine views of the sect:

> Now some people say, "If I possess God and God's love, I can do anything I want". They do not understand these words correctly. As long as you can do anything against God and his commandments, you do not have the love of God ... The person who is established in God's will and God's love finds it delightful to do all the things that are pleasing to God and to avoid doing those that are against God.[55]

Whereas the brothers and sisters of the Free Spirit did not recognise any obligation to outsiders, Eckhart proclaimed a universal ethic that in moral terms seems excessive:

> If you love yourself, you love all men as yourself. As long as you love one single person less than yourself, you have never really loved yourself.[56]

Again, in contrast to the Free Spirit teaching, he recognises the deference and obedience due to those in authority: to our "father and mother that we should honour them; [and] all those, too, who have spiritual power should be honoured and treated with great respect".[57]

their colours, see R. Manstetten, *Esse est Deus* (Freiburg im Breisgau, 1993), pp. 389-93.

[53] Sermon 29 in *Deutsche Werke*, ed. Quint, 2:73-89; *Meister Eckhart*, ed. McGinn, pp. 287-91.

[54] *Deutsche Werke*, ed. Quint, 2:78; *Meister Eckhart*, ed. McGinn, p. 288.

[55] *Deutsche Werke*, ed. Quint, 2:78; *Meister Eckhart*, ed. McGinn, p. 288.

[56] Sermon 12 in *Deutsche Werke*, ed. Quint, 1:195; *Meister Eckhart*, ed. McGinn, p. 268.

[57] Sermon 51 in *Deutsche Werke*, ed. Quint, 2:468; *German Sermons*, ed. Walshe, 2:250.

Eckhart's explanation of the sacrament of the Eucharist to unbelievers begins in simple terms. A human being develops from the food provided by his parents. We are all aware that this development is effected within our natural potentiality; above and beyond this we need to be aware that God can effect the transformation of the eucharistic bread into the body of Christ.[58] He leaves aside the theories of transubstantiation and relies on God's omnipotence as his decisive argument.

In reasoning with the members of the Free Spirit Eckhart exposed himself to the danger of appearing to ignore certain important distinctions; but the initial charges against him were made by a malevolent group among his own brethren and not by the ecclesiastical hierarchy. The Cologne Dominicans, Herman de Summa and William de Nidecke, accused him of offences against the order's constitutions and made depositions against him during a visitation by Nicholas de Argentina; the visitator responded by charging the two friars with falsely accusing one of their brethren.[59] An anonymous Dutch tract "Meister Eckhart and the layman" supports Eckhart's case by claiming that he was the protector of ordinary lay people of good will who were denied the possibility of spiritual competence by other less sympathetic Dominicans.[60] Henry Suso's defence of the Meister in his *Buchli der Warheit* revealed that Eckhart was engaged in discussion with the Free Spirit.[61]

Meister Eckhart and other German Dominicans faced a great pastoral challenge in their dealings with the new spiritual movements of their day. Whereas most of their contemporaries did little more than quote Catholic doctrine to the religious and lay members of these groups and lose patience with them if they failed

[58] *Deutsche Werke*, ed. Quint, 2:474-75; *German Sermons*, ed. Walshe, 1:253.

[59] W. Trusen, *Der Prozess gegen Meister Eckhart* (Paderborn, 1988) gives a convincing reappraisal of the trial based on a precise reinterpretation of the sources in the light of the canon law of that time. For a condensed and updated version see W. Trusen, "Meister Eckhart vor seinen Richtern und Zensoren", in *Meister Eckhart*, ed. Jacobi, pp. 335-52.

[60] F. Schweitzer, *Meister Eckhart und der Laie* (Berlin, 1997), p. lxxii.

[61] Henry Suso, *Henricus Suso, Das Buch der Wahrheit* ed. R. Blumrich and L. Sturlese (Hamburg, 1993), pp. 56, 64.

to accept it unquestioningly, Eckhart was sympathetic to their justified longing for a deeper personal faith: he was willing to reason with them in order to win them over.

Merit Ranking, the Religious Orders, and the Parisian Faculty of Theology in the Later Middle Ages

Thomas Sullivan

Students at the late medieval university of Paris beginning work toward the master's degree in theology embarked on a long, arduous, and expensive programme, lasting many years and consisting of three stages. The first, in which the student was sometimes called an *auditor*, demanded a number of years of passive reception through the reading and study of required texts and attendance at lectures on those texts. The second involved a period of apprenticeship or student teaching and disputing known as the baccalaureate. This stage included three steps; the student of theology was first a *baccalarius biblicus* or *baccalarius cursor*, then a *baccalarius sententiarius*, and finally a *baccalarius formatus*. In the third stage, the student's prolonged process of work and study culminated in the licentiate and inception as a master.[1] On the appointed day, candidates for the *licentia in theologia* gathered in the *aula* of the bishop's palace, where the chancellor of Paris preached a sermon and conferred the licence as each candidate knelt before him. This was the renowned *licentia ubique docendi*, the

[1] William J. Courtenay, "Programs of Study and Genres of Scholastic Theological Production in the Fourteenth Century", in *Manuels, programmes de cours et techniques d'enseignement dans les universités médiévales*, ed. Jacqueline Hamesse (Louvain-la-Neuve, 1994), pp. 325-350 at p. 330.

permission to teach here and everywhere in the world, conferred in the name of the Father, the Son, and of the Holy Spirit and on the authority of the apostles Peter and Paul and of the Holy See.

In conferring the licence, the chancellor received each graduate according to a merit ranking. Faculty of theology statutes called for the chancellor to follow strictly a composite ranking arrived at by a secret ballot of the regent masters of theology.[2] The significance of ordering the graduates was that rank was understood to bespeak academic excellence and that rank determined precedence in subsequent ceremonies and examinations. Moreover, because the university's register of licentiates listed the graduates in the order in which they were licensed, rank remained a matter of permanent record.[3]

A form of this register of licentiates is presented in the *Registrum Facultatis theologiae. Ordo licentiatorum 1373-1694*,[4] redacted in the mid-seventeenth century by Philippe Bouvot, beadle of the faculty of theology.[5] This work records the licences granted by the faculty of theology between 1373 and 1694, listing – in order

[2] Heinrich Denifle and Émile Chatelain, eds, *Chartularium universitatis parisiensis*, 4 vols (Paris, 1889-97) 2:683 (no. 24), 684-85 (no. 25); James K. Farge, *Orthodoxy and Reform in Early Reformation France: The Faculty of Theology of Paris 1500-1543*, Studies in Medieval and Reformation Thought, 32 (Leiden, 1978), p. 26.

[3] Alan E. Bernstein, *Pierre d'Ailly and the Blanchard Affair: University and Chancellor of Paris at the Beginning of the Great Schism*, Studies in Medieval and Reformation Thought, 24 (Leiden, 1978), p. 102.

[4] Paris, Bibliothèque nationale MS lat 5657-A.

[5] In preparing the database which is the foundation of this study, Bouvot's register served as the main source, supplemented and corrected by the following: *Catalogue des licenciés de la Faculté de Théologie de Paris depuis 1373-1774* (Paris, Bibl. nat. MS lat 15440); *Chartularium universitatis parisiensis*; Robert Marichal, ed., *Le Livre des Prieurs de Sorbonne (1431-1485)* (Paris, 1987); John Barry Weber, ed., "The Register of the Beadle (Receipts and Expenses) of the Faculty of Theology of Paris from 1449-1465. (Editing of Text of Paris, Bibl. nat. ms 5657-C, folio 1 recto-94 verso)" (unpublished Ph.D. dissertation, University of Notre Dame, 1975); Henri-Bernard Maitre, S. J., "Les 'Théologastres' de l'Université de Paris au Temps d'Érasme et de Rabelais (1496-1536)", *Bibliothèque d'humanisme et renaissance* 27 (1965), 248-64.

of merit – the names of the *licentiati* (with variant spellings and aliases), the date of inception for those proceeding on to the magistracy, the religious order where appropriate, college affiliation for many seculars, regional origin for some, and notations concerning the further career for many of the clerics licensed.[6]

The register thus furnishes the historian of the late medieval university of Paris with a wealth of biographical information regarding the 1017 clerics licensed in theology between 1374 and 1500. Analysis of the data provided by the register enables the historian not only to assess both the quantity and relative quality of the various groups and subgroups to which those licensed were aggregated but also to answer other significant questions about their academic careers and achievement. While this paper has as an important focus the academic accomplishments of the monastic orders, comparing and contrasting their accomplishments with those of the secular clerics, it hopes as well to rescue the monks from the shadow of the friars, to which they have been traditionally relegated in university histories.

For both assessment and comparative purposes, it is possible to distinguish individuals in the sample first between secular clerics and regulars. Those designated regulars may then be classified in turn according to their *conversatio* or way of life (canonical, monastic, mendicant, and other). Each *conversatio* may be further subdivided according to religious order represented, including the orders of regular canons, monks living according to the rule of St Benedict (Benedictine, Cluniac, and Cistercian), and several orders of mendicant friars.

It is important to note also that the *Ordo licentiatorum* is wanting information for the years 1414 through 1421, years exceptionally troublesome for both the city and university of Paris, years of warfare, brigandage, famine, hunger, and slaughter. The city's difficulties may explain the discontinuity in the licentiate

[6] James K. Farge, *Biographical Register of Paris Doctors of Theology, 1500-1536*, Subsidia Mediaevalia, 10 (Toronto, 1980), p. 457.

records.[7] This lacuna, unfortunate as it is, provides us with the opportunity, again for comparative and assessment purposes, to differentiate between two periods: Period I, which covers 1374-1413, and Period II for the years 1422-1500.

The *Ordo licentiatorum* shows that approximately four out of ten *licentiati* (43%) were secular clerics and six out of ten (57%) professed members of religious orders. A comparison of the figures provided by Bouvot's register with computations from other periods in the history of the university of Paris proves informative. Palemon Glorieux's *Répertoire*, for instance, identifies 286 masters of theology incepting between 1167 and 1320, 46% secular and 54% regular masters. The composition of this earlier body of masters is thus quite similar to that of the clerics licensed between 1374 and 1500.[8]

A comparison of frequency distributions from Period I (1374-1411) and Period II (1422-1500), however, shows an increase from the first to the second periods of ten points in the percentage of secular clerics (37% to 47%) and a concomitant decrease in the percentage of regular clerics (63% to 53%) comprising the body of *licentiati*. The increasing secularisation of the Parisian faculty of theology from Period I to Period II prepares us for James K. Farge's prosopography of Parisian theological masters from 1500-1536, which reveals a reversal in the proportions established for 1167-1320 and 1374-1500. Farge's register names 474 graduates, of these 55% are noted as secular clerics and 45% regular.[9]

[7] See Charles Jourdain, *L'Université de Paris à l'époque de la domination anglaise* (Paris, 1870) and Jean Favier, *Nouvelle histoire de Paris: Paris au XVe siècle, 1380-1500* (Paris, 1974).

[8] These figures are reported in Reuven Avi-Yonah, "Career Trends of Parisian Masters of Theology, 1200-1320", *History of Universities* 6 (1986-87), 47 and are based on the work of Palemon Glorieux, *Répertoire des Maîtres en Théologie de Paris au XIIIe siècle*, 2 vols (Paris, 1933-34) and V. Doucet, "Maîtres franciscains de Paris: Supplément au *Répertoire des maîtres en théologie de Paris au XIIIe siècle* de M. le Cha. P. Glorieux", *Archivum Franciscanum Historicum*, 27 (1935), 531-64.

[9] Farge, *Orthodoxy and Reform*, p. 56, Table 1.

Of the total sample of 1017 licensed clerics, 57% were regular clerics, that is, professed members of religious orders. Three-quarters of the religious granted licentiates between 1374 and 1500 belonged to the mendicant orders and over one-fifth to the monastic orders.[10] The number of mendicant religious licensed increased by eight percentage points between the first and second periods while monastic licentiates decreased by the same amount. This reduction in monastic theologians is clearly attributable to the Benedictine monks (declining from Period I to Period II by 12%), rather than the Cluniacs or the Cistercians, whose percentages increased by eight and four percent respectively in the second period. It should be noted, however, that the Benedictines expended more of their scholastic energies in the faculty of canon law than in the faculty of theology, graduating seventy-four licentiates in canon law at Paris between 1374 and 1500 and twenty-five for the period 1422-1500.[11]

Who were the best and the brightest among those licensed? Because the *Ordo licentiatorum* presents each licentiate's position in his class as determined by the masters, the merit rank or class standing of each of the *licentiati* can be ascertained, and that position converted into a percentile rank as well as a quartile rank. The upper quartile is defined as the 75th percentile, with only 25% of the measures above the upper quartile; the lower quartile as the 25th percentile, with 75% of the measures above the lower quartile; and finally the interquartile range as the set of measures lying

[10] Because the canons regular and the non-monastic, non-mendicant religious offered relatively insignificant numbers of their orders as candidates for the licentiate (only twenty or 4% of the total licenced), they are not included in the following discussion.

[11] See Thomas Sullivan, *Benedictine Monks at the University of Paris, A.D. 1229-1500: A Biographical Register*, Education and Society in the Middle Ages and Renaissance, 4 (Leiden, 1995), pp. 419-20; "Benedictine Masters of the University of Paris in the Late Middle Ages: Patterns of Recruitment", *Vivarium*, 31 (1993), 226-40; and the forthcoming "Benedictine Masters of the Medieval University of Paris: Careers and Regency", *Medieval Prosopography* 18 (1998).

between the upper and lower quartiles, or the middle 50% of the measures.[12]

Of the 1006 clerics ranked by the faculty of theology,[13] over a third (37%) of the seculars achieved upper quartile status; a little over a tenth (11%) of the regular clerics succeeded in earning upper quartile placement. Lower quartile assignment was made to only 17% of the secular clerics and to over a third (37%) of the regular clerics. The difference in achievement intensifies when contrasting the first and second periods. The number of secular clerics assigned to the upper quartile jumped from 30% in Period I to 39% in Period II. The number of regulars in the upper quartile of their classes dropped from 17% in Period I to a mere 8% in Period II. Appointment to the lower quartile declined from 21% to 15% for secular clerics and rose from 33% to 39% for regulars.

And where were the best and the brightest located according to *conversatio* and religious order? The regent masters assigned fully one-fifth of the monks to the upper quartile, and only a tenth of the mendicants. When considering the lower quartile, we find a little over a third of the monks assigned there, and 38% of the mendicants. A comparison of Period I with Period II shows both monks and mendicants losing points in the percentages assigned to the upper quartile: monks decreasing from 27% to 14% and mendicants from 13% to 7%. Nomination to the lower quartile for the monastic licentiates dropped slightly, from 36% to 33%; that of their mendicant brethren increased considerably, from 32% to 41%.

William J. Courtenay suggests that the mendicant orders in the fourteenth and fifteenth centuries increasingly used the doctoral programme at Paris as a means for grooming and furnishing with credentials their administrative leadership, and that the selection of

[12] David H. Voelker and Peter Z. Orton, *Statistics* (Lincoln, Neb., 1993), p. 39.

[13] The discrepancy between the number of clerics licensed (1017) and ranked (1006) results from the presence in the sample of clerics whose licences were either *bullata* (granted at special papal request) or granted *de gratia facultatis*. Those awarded these special licences were not ranked by the faculty and therefore cannot be counted among those ranked.

candidates for higher studies had become highly political.[14] Mendicant students may not have been assigned to the university because of their academic potential or excellence but because of the administrative needs of their orders and the political pull of their mentors.

Turning to the individual religious orders, we see that the faculty of theology, when ranking the monks according to merit, assigned upper quartile standing to 17% of the Benedictines, 19% of the Cluniacs, and 22% of the Cistercians. When ranking the mendicants, the masters assigned upper quartile rank to only 7% of the Franciscans, 8% of the Augustinian Hermits, 10% to the Dominicans, and 11% to the Carmelites. While the victor's crown can be awarded to the Cistercians among the monks and the Carmelites among the mendicants, it should be noted that the percentage of Cistercians assigned to the upper quartile is double that of the Carmelite friars.

Lower quartile status was awarded the monastic orders in a rather tight cluster: 35% for the Benedictines, 36% for the Cluniacs, and 33% for the Cistercians. The Franciscans saw 37% of their *licentiati* assigned to the lower quartile, the Augustinian Hermits 38%, and the Dominicans a surprisingly high 42%. The faculty of theology awarded the Carmelite friars the fewest lower quartile positions among both the monks and the mendicants, only 31%. It should be pointed out, however, that in comparison with the regulars only 17% of the secular clerics were assigned to the lower quartile.

After such a welter of percentage figures, it would perhaps be useful to summarise the responses to the questions: Who were the best and the brightest and where were they to be found? Between the seculars and regulars, the masters of the faculty of theology accorded the seculars the higher ranking. Comparing the monks with the mendicants, the theologians judged the monks to be the brighter. And among the nine monastic and mendicant orders

[14] William J. Courtenay, "The Mendicant Studia at Paris: The Lectorate Program", to appear in *The Medieval Church: Universities, Heresy and the Religious Life. Essays in Honor of Gordon Leff*, ed. P. Biller and R. B. Dobson (London, 1997).

represented, Cistercians monks earned the highest number of upper quartile assignments.

Jacques Verger suggests that many *licentiati* did not complete the last stage of their education by incepting as masters or doctors[15] because this title was far more costly than the ordinary degree and was indispensable only for those who, since they wished to teach, found it necessary to affiliate with the college of masters or doctors.[16] Bouvot's register provides us with the opportunity to determine inception rates for the 674 theologians licensed at Paris between 1422-1500 and to ascertain the role merit ranking played in achieving the magistracy.[17]

Of the 674 clerics licensed in the second period, 583 incepted as masters of theology, presenting an overall inception rate of 86%. Farge's study of inception rates for Parisian theologians in the first third of the sixteenth century reveals a higher rate of inception. Of the 474 clerics licensed during the years 1500-1536, only twenty-seven failed to proceed to the doctorate – for an inception rate of 94%.[18]

The 315 secular clerics incepted at a rate of 84% and the 359 regulars at 89%. The percentage of monks incepting is 86%, that of the mendicant clergy 89%. Among the particular religious orders represented in these two *conversatio* groupings, we find the highest

[15] The three separate parts to the final act of the graduation – the theological inception – included disputations, lectures, and other ceremonies. For a full description of the inception ceremonies, see Lowrie J. Daly, S. J., *The Medieval University, 1200-1400* (New York, 1961), pp. 147-50 and Gordon Leff, *Paris and Oxford Universities in the Thirteenth and Fourteenth Centuries: An Institutional and Intellectual History* (New York, 1968), pp. 169-71.

[16] Jacques Verger, "Teachers", in, *Universities in the Middle Ages*, ed. Hilde de Ridder-Symoens (vol. 1 of *A History of the University in Europe*) (Cambridge, 1992), pp. 144-68 at p. 147. See also Jacques Verger, "Le coût des grades: droits et frais d'examen dans les universités du Midi de la France à la fin du Moyen Age", in *The Economic and Material Frame of the Mediaeval University*, ed. A. L. Gabriel (Notre Dame, 1977), pp. 19-36.

[17] Unfortunately, Bouvot provided the inception dates sporadically for Period I, though consistently for Period II. For this reason, only the inception rates for the second period can be considered reliable.

[18] Farge, *Orthodoxy and Reform*, p. 27.

inception rates among the Franciscans and the Cistercians, both at 95%. Those incepting at the lowest rates were the Cluniac monks at 70%, the Augustinian Hermits at 73%, the Carmelite friars at 80%, and finally by the Benedictine monks incepting at a rate of 82%.

It may be useful to distinguish inception rates according to quartile assignment. The rate of inception for the second period's population was highest among the *licentiati* assigned by the masters to the upper quartile, at 95%, and lowest among those awarded lower quartile status, at 78%. Seculars awarded upper quartile ranking incepted at a rate of 95% and regulars at 97%. Regulars assigned to the lower quartile incepted at a rate of 85%; seculars, however, managed only 60%.

It appears from these figures that a lower ranking may have influenced either the ability or the desire for seculars thus ranked to move on to the magistracy, perhaps having a negative effect on their ability to attract financial support to cover the high costs of inception. The higher figures for the inception of religious may result from the fact that religious had the advantage of their orders' corporate wealth and support as well as particular legislation restricting inception extravagance.[19]

In 1334, Robert Holcot, a Dominican friar writing probably at Oxford, asserted that, "As Christ entered the immortal Jerusalem riding upon an ass, so the school of theology is carried for the most part not by the great and powerful or the rich, but by the poor religious".[20] Holcot was alluding to the fact that in the first part of the fourteenth century, university theological faculties were dominated both quantitatively and qualitatively by the mendicants

[19] The Cluniac general chapter, for instance, imposed a tax of two hundred florins on all the houses of the order in April 1367 so that the expenses for the inception of Guillelmus de Pomeriis, grand prior of Cluny, could be met [Gaston Charvin, O. S. B., ed., *Statuts, chapitres généraux et visites de l'ordre de Cluny*, 9 vols and supplement (Paris, 1965-1982), 4:45]. The statutes published for the Parisian Collège de Saint-Bernard in 1493 by the Cistercian order attempted to restrict such expenses by establishing a scale of payments for various occasions and limiting the number of invited guests [Michel Félibien, *Histoire de la ville de Paris*, 5 vols (Paris, 1725), 3:171-72].

[20] Beryl Smalley, *English Friars and Antiquity in the Early Fourteenth Century* (Oxford, 1960), p. 31.

and perhaps by the other religious orders which by then had founded houses of study at universities throughout Europe.[21]

This brief investigation into Bouvot's *Ordo licentiatorum* perhaps bears out R. B. Dobson's suggestion that the presence of monks and friars at *studium generale* was intended less to enhance their individual learning than to augment the general influence of their respective orders.[22] While the Parisian faculty of theology in the later middle ages was indeed dominated in quantity by the so-called poor religious, in quality – at least as indicated by merit ranking – the secular theologians held sway. The ascendancy of the secular masters, initiated in the late fourteenth century by the extraordinary careers in teaching and administration of such as Pierre d'Ailly and Jean Gerson,[23] would continue throughout the fifteenth century until both number and quality were in the hands of the secular clergy.

[21] C. H. Lawrence, *The Friars: The Impact of the Early Mendicant Movement on Western Society* (London, 1994), p. 226.

[22] R. B. Dobson, "The Religious Orders 1370-1540", in *The History of the University of Oxford, vol. 2: Late Medieval Oxford*, ed. J. I. Catto and Ralph Evans (Oxford, 1992), p. 541.

[23] Both Pierre d'Ailly and Jean Gerson were ranked first in their promotions by the faculty of theology, the former in 1381 and the latter in 1392 (Paris, Bibl. nat. MS lat. 5657-A, fol. 9r and 11r respectively).